Invitations to Diplomacy

This series was launched by DiploFoundation in 2018. It aims to provide authors with the opportunity to publish introductory works on any important diplomatic subject, and to make them as accessible as possible in terms of style and costs.

Also by G. R. Berridge

THE DIPLOMACY OF ANCIENT GREECE: A Short Introduction

DIPLOMACY, SATIRE AND THE VICTORIANS:
The Life and Writings of E. C. Grenville-Murray

EMBASSIES IN ARMED CONFLICT

THE PALGRAVE MACMILLAN DICTIONARY OF DIPLOMACY (*with Lorna Lloyd*),
Third Edition

THE COUNTER-REVOLUTION IN DIPLOMACY AND OTHER ESSAYS

DIPLOMACY: Theory and Practice, Sixth Edition

BRITISH DIPLOMACY IN TURKEY, 1583 TO THE PRESENT:
A Study in the Evolution of the Resident Embassy

TILKIDOM AND THE OTTOMAN EMPIRE:
The Letters of Gerald Fitzmaurice to George Lloyd, 1906–15

GERALD FITZMAURICE (1865–1939), CHIEF DRAGOMAN
OF THE BRITISH EMBASSY IN TURKEY

DIPLOMATIC CLASSICS: Selected texts from Commynes to Vattel

DIPLOMATIC THEORY FROM MACHIAVELLI TO KISSINGER
(*with Maurice Keens-Soper and T. G. Otte*)

INTERNATIONAL POLITICS: States, Power and Conflict since 1945, Third Edition

TALKING TO THE ENEMY: How States without 'Diplomatic Relations' Communicate

AN INTRODUCTION TO INTERNATIONAL RELATIONS (*with D. Heater*)

SOUTH AFRICA, THE COLONIAL POWERS AND 'AFRICAN DEFENCE':
The Rise and Fall of the White Entente, 1948–60

RETURN TO THE UN: UN Diplomacy in Regional Conflicts

THE POLITICS OF THE SOUTH AFRICA RUN: European Shipping and Pretoria

DIPLOMACY AT THE UN (*co-editor with A. Jennings*)

ECONOMIC POWER IN ANGLO-SOUTH AFRICAN DIPLOMACY:
Simonstown, Sharpeville and After

DIPLOMACY AND SECRET SERVICE

A Short Introduction

G. R. Berridge

Emeritus Professor of International Politics,
University of Leicester, UK
and
Senior Fellow, DiploFoundation

www.diplomacy.edu

Cover design by: Viktor Mijatovic (DiploFoundation)

ISBN: 979-8-9870052-3-1

Published by: Diplo US (2022)

For Mina

Contents

Preface and Acknowledgements

The ideas in this short introduction have their distant origins in the chapter I wrote on secret intelligence for my textbook, *International Politics*, first published in 1987, but more especially in a stimulating discussion paper called 'Diplomacy and Intelligence' published in March 1998. This was the work of that finest of scholar-intelligence professionals, Michael Herman [www], then retired, for the University of Leicester's Centre for the Study of Diplomacy, of which I was at the time director. (The paper drew on materials from his major work, *Intelligence Power in Peace and War*, published two years earlier, and subsequently appeared in the journal *Diplomacy & Statecraft*.) Michael also visited us and spoke to my students. Raising the question of the relationship between diplomacy and intelligence as he did, albeit rather briefly, sparked my interest but it was not until I was planning the expanded Fifth Edition of my graduate textbook, *Diplomacy: Theory and Practice*, published in 2015, that it belatedly occurred to me to probe the question more fully with a new chapter called simply 'Secret Intelligence'.
By this time the academic study of this subject was well-established and a great wealth of revealing material had become available for research, whether in consequence of freedom of information legislation, parliamentary investigations prompted by secret service excesses, or revelations by defectors and disgruntled intelligence officers, among others. This book builds on my textbook chapter on the subject and, as far as I know, is the only extended treatment of what Michael Herman called 'the interface' between diplomacy and intelligence. Such neglect is the more surprising in light of the massive public attention periodically received by the activities of 'spooks' in embassies or, thanks to the Saudi government, in consular missions.

To avoid over-cluttering the text, as a rule I have restricted the footnotes to parenthetical additions not worthy of highlighting in a box, and to sources for quotations as well as occasional statements that might otherwise raise an eyebrow. The list of references at the end of each chapter is designed chiefly as a guide to further reading but also indicates the sources on which it has relied most heavily. A full list of all of the works on which I have drawn is to be found in the 'References' in the endmatter.

I have tried to limit citations of recently published online press articles to those published by the shrinking number of newspapers that do not have a paywall, which as often as not means *The Guardian*. As it happens, this is also the most trusted newspaper in Britain and the most-read quality news outlet, according to figures released by the Publishers' Audience Measurement Company in December 2018. Where possible, and other things being equal, I cite online rather than print sources. As in earlier editions, I have avoided providing URLs for such sources, partly because they are often so long, partly because they tend to change or disappear, and partly because it is usually easy enough to find a web resource via a search engine; I simply add '[www]' to a reference available on the Internet at the time of writing, although a few might be behind paywalls.

With the exceptions of the 'Staff of British Embassy Moscow' and 'The Common Cuckoo', which are the author's photographs from works not covered by copyright (*FO List* and Johns's *British Birds in their Haunts*, 1911), and the cover of the Penguin-published *Mitrokhin Archive*, all of the illustrations in this book were obtained via Wikimedia Commons and are therefore in the public domain. The only additional explanations or attributions properly required, are as follows: photographs of Walsingham and Wicquefort portraits – in the public domain in the USA because it was published (or registered with the U.S. Copyright Office) before January 1, 1924; Canaris photo – German Federal Archives, licensed under the Creative Commons [www], Attribution-Share Alike 3.0 Germany [www]; Bandar–Putin meeting [www] and licensed under the Creative Commons Attribution 4.0 [www] + Creative Commons Attribution 3.0 Unported [www]; Moussa Koussa – photo by magharebia (Flickr @Magharebia) and licensed under the Creative Commons [www], Attribution 2.0 Generic [www].

I am grateful to Hannah Slavik for supporting this project and to Mina Mudrić and her colleagues Viktor Mijatović and Aleksandar Nedeljkov in the publishing wing of DiploFoundation for their expertise in design and production.

G. R. B., Leicester, January 2019

List of Abbreviations

CIA	Central Intelligence Agency
CREST	CIA Records Search Tool
DNI	Director of National Intelligence [US]
DPRK	Democratic People's Republic of Korea
FAS	Federation of American Scientists
FVEY	Five Eyes' alliance
GCHQ	Government Communications Headquarters [British]
GRU	Glavnoye Razvedyvatelnoye Upravleniye [Russian – formerly Soviet – military intelligence]
Humint	Human intelligence/espionage
ISCP	Intelligence and Security Committee of Parliament [British]
NOC	Non-Official Cover (aka 'illegal')
NSA	National Security Agency [US]
ODNB	*Oxford Dictionary of National Biography* (Oxford: Oxford University Press)
PCO	Passport Control Officer
PNGing	Declaring a diplomat persona non grata – no longer welcome
S&T	Science and Technology
Sigint	Signals intelligence
SIS	Secret Intelligence Service [British; aka MI6]
SVR	Sluzhba Vneshney Razvedki [successor to the foreign wing of the KGB – Russian External Intelligence Service]
VCDR	Vienna Convention on Diplomatic Relations, 18 April 1961
WMD	weapons of mass destruction

List of Boxes

List of Illustrations

Introduction

Intelligence officers working under diplomatic protection are rarely out of the news for long, and the last two years have been no exception. In August 2017, the Soviet consulate-general in San Francisco was closed down on Washington's insistence because the eavesdropping on Silicon Valley by its secret intelligence residency (*rezidentura*) had become intolerable. Less than a year later, in March 2018, Britain and other states expelled between them over 150 Russian diplomats alleged to be intelligence officers in retaliation for the attempt by two operatives of Russian military intelligence to murder the defector, Sergei Skripal, with the nerve agent Novichok, in Shrewsbury, England. It can safely be assumed that the equivalent number of diplomats expelled from Moscow in response to these actions also included intelligence officers. And on 2 October 2018 the dissident Saudi journalist, Jamal Khashoggi, was duped into entering the Saudi Consulate-General in Istanbul and there murdered in grisly fashion by a hit squad from Riyadh which included intelligence officers. Throughout this whole period strong circumstantial evidence was also accumulating that the President of the United States, no less, is an agent of influence for Russia whose cultivation began in 1986 and was assisted by intelligence officers in the Soviet/Russian missions in New York and Washington.

The instances in the foregoing paragraph all show a continuing intimacy between the worlds of traditional diplomacy and secret intelligence in the twenty-first century. But how did the relationship between diplomacy and secret intelligence come about? How did the role of ambassadors in the running of agents evolve? What was the impact on the relationship of the bureaucratization of secret intelligence that began in the late nineteenth century? Is diplomatic immunity, as is sometimes supposed, the only reason why intelligence officers cluster in embassies and consulates? What do their diplomatic landlords think about their secret tenants today and what if anything can the spooks do to repay the ambassadors for their lodgings? These are among the key questions this work will consider.

1   The Ambassador as Agent-runner

Until well into the nineteenth century, the central figure in secret intelligence was usually the head of a diplomatic mission, whether the ambassador who ran an embassy or the minister in charge of the more lowly ranked – and much more numerous – legation.[1] In the first centuries of the modern state, however, notwithstanding the fact that even then the diplomats' role was significant, the chief responsibility for secret intelligence was sometimes assumed by an individual at home: a 'spymaster'. Therefore, this chapter will begin by examining this species – so loved by television drama-documentaries – before proceeding to look at the role of ambassadors as agent-runners, together with the part played in their schemes by the lowly consul.

The spymaster

Until the eighteenth century, foreign intelligence operations – other than those conducted independently by armies and navies or by post office interceptions – were sometimes directed chiefly by an intimate of a ruler. Such a person created and ran a network of agents with whom his relationship was essentially personal. Among such well-known 'spymasters' were Cardinal Richelieu (1585–1642), first minister of King Louis XIII of France; Axel Oxenstierna (1583–1654), lord high chancellor of Sweden; John Thurloe (1616–68), secretary of state during Cromwell's English protectorate; and, most famous of all in the English-speaking world, Sir Francis Walsingham (Box 1.1), who served the Protestant Queen of England, Elizabeth I, a monarch who faced periodic threats of invasion from Catholic Spain and lived in constant fear of assassination and Catholic rebellion at home. There were national variations but the kinds of agent employed in Walsingham's network were fairly typical of those of other states. Some were employed in 'special' activities such as black propaganda, as well as in the acquisition of secrets by observation, eavesdropping, and theft of letters and other documents.

      Some spymasters were very successful but the scheme had serious dangers. For one thing, interpretation of the significance of the intelligence obtained was always likely to be weak because the prejudices of the spymaster – who was also a top policy-maker – would go unchallenged, unless a rival for influence at court set up another network, as did the doomed Earl of Essex in competition with Robert Cecil at the court of Elizabeth I. For another, there was the risk that the intelligence would not be usefully distributed

---

[1]   For the sake of brevity, I shall henceforward follow the common practice of using the term 'ambassador' for the head of any resident diplomatic mission.

because it was regarded as personal property and vital to the spymaster's influence with his sovereign. The most serious limitation of this system, however, was that because the spymaster tended to be focussed on a specific problem as well as holding his agents only by personal loyalty, the risk was always high that the network would dissolve with the abatement of the problem or his death or political eclipse. It was perhaps in part for these reasons – especially the last – that, although the system lingered at least to the end of the eighteenth century,[2] it began to give way to the resident mission after this institution became the fulcrum upon which diplomacy turned in the course of the sixteenth century and the obvious point for the regular, official collection of secret intelligence.

Box 1.1 Sir Francis Walsingham: Spymaster of Elizabeth I

Sir Francis Walsingham (c.1532–1590), previously a successful diplomat, was appointed a principal secretary to Queen Elizabeth I of England in 1573. Building on the secret intelligence work of his master, William Cecil (Lord Burghley after 1571), and in order to supplement the reports he received from English ambassadors, in the early 1570s Walsingham expanded both the number and distribution of intelligence-gatherers in the English network. (His responsibilities also included counter-intelligence at home.) Assisted by the fluency in French and Italian and many foreign contacts acquired in the five years he spent abroad during the reign of the previous English monarch (a Catholic), he is said by his admiring late nineteenth century biographer to have 'had in his pay fifty-three private agents in foreign courts, besides eighteen spies who performed functions that could not be officially defined' (Lee, 'Walsingham'). They were found in France, Germany, Italy, the Netherlands, Spain and even in the Ottoman Empire. His network consisted chiefly of:

- 'intelligencers', freelancers who sold information to the highest bidder
- couriers, whose day job required not only courage and resourcefulness but also some knowledge of foreign lands and languages
- English merchants at home and abroad, who not only supplied intelligence but also served as go-betweens to pay the intelligencers and handle communications with them, and
- disaffected Catholics, including captured priests, who could sometimes be 'turned' as the price of release from imprisonment and torture, and planted in exile communities, Catholic seminaries abroad, and so on

At his London home, Walsingham had a personal secretariat, the members of which helped him to run his agents and were sometimes themselves sent abroad for this purpose. They also helped him to analyse their product, intercept and read correspondence without alerting the addressee, create and break codes, plan what would now be called 'covert actions'; for example, kidnapping the papal legate to France, black propaganda and forged documents. Sometimes, members of his staff also undertook missions of secret reconnaissance abroad and sensitive diplomatic missions.

The costs of Walsingham's operation were met chiefly (but grudgingly) by the Queen and were particularly heavy as the threat increased from Spain, but he had to bear a significant portion of the expenses himself. His network had many successes but his crowning achievement was the advance intelligence it supplied on the size and armaments of the Spanish Armada, which contributed to its defeat in 1588. Dying in 1590, Walsingham pre-deceased Burghley, whose son Robert subsequently became Elizabeth's chief spymaster.

---

[2]   There is a strong whiff of Walsingham about the agent-running of Adam de Cardonnel, chief clerk at the British War Office and secretary to the Duke of Marlborough while on campaign in the War of the Spanish Succession, Rule, 'Review of *Espions et Ambassadeurs*', p. 739; as also about the network run in the 1770s by William Eden, under-secretary in the Foreign Office's Northern Department (which included American-born British subjects working as double agents) against the American mission in Paris during the War of American Independence, Bemis, 'British secret service and the French-American alliance'.

The resident mission

The resident diplomatic mission was established in Italy in the turbulent conditions of the late fifteenth century and before long spread through Europe as far as Moscow and Constantinople. Only through long residence, it was realised, could a diplomat gain sufficient knowledge of his posting and make enough contacts to provide full and reliable reports on political, military and commercial developments of importance, and this was the chief reason for the appearance of this new institution; its other functions were secondary. Further evidence of the anxiety for information of those who sent them was that ambassadors were also encouraged to mix in the diplomatic corps and engage in periodic correspondence with diplomatic colleagues at neighbouring posts, thereby not only gaining more local knowledge but also learning more of wider affairs. The information-gathering potential of missions was increased further when it had satellite consular posts that were required to report – with some exceptions – not directly to home but to the ambassador.

Because it was known why they were being set up, some states were reluctant to admit resident missions until they realised that it was unflattering not to have their attention and that in any case this was the price of establishing abroad their own envoys. But wariness of their chief purpose was never shaken off and this meant that ambassadors always had to stress that they were not 'spies'; that, unlike such unsavoury individuals, they gathered their information only by open and legitimate means. Nevertheless, in light of the priority usually given to this task – and the urgency added to it at moments of crisis – it was a natural step to seek concealed information as well. Unlike intelligencers, merchants and others, ambassadors were also uniquely well placed to contemplate this with some equanimity: first, because of their ready access to those with power and authority and thus with the secrets most worth penetrating; second, because they had experience of sending information home as quickly and securely as possible; and third, because – should they be caught – the substantial immunity from civil and criminal prosecution they enjoyed under the developing law of nations usually meant that the worst they would suffer would be expulsion. This is why heads of mission became the new agent-runners, developing their own networks to acquire sensitive information by surreptitious means – and supplied with more or less generous funds from home to support the work. This was markedly the case in wartime and in situations such as those prevailing in the United Provinces of the Netherlands in the mid-1780s where external powers were engaged in an intense struggle for influence that could break out into war; and also in peacetime at unfriendly courts, where information was less easy to obtain.

The changing role of the ambassador

From the sixteenth century to the first decades of the nineteenth, some ambassadors were intimately involved not only in launching and directing but also in carrying out secret intelligence work, whether designed to obtain information, recruit agents of influence, undermine foreign enemies or provide material support to foreign friends. With the noun in the phrase loosely construed, many truly were 'honourable spies'.[3] The most effective device for these purposes was money: small payments to minor agents, large 'bribes' to important foreigner ministers and officials, most suitable to the latter purpose being a regular 'pension'.[4] The need to lay out 'gratuities and secret pensions' – albeit 'with artifice' and alertness to the risk of being duped by the beneficiaries – was repeatedly urged by the theorist of the French system of diplomacy, François de Callières, no doubt because he was afraid that most ambassadors spent 'much more willingly in keeping a great number of horses and idle servants.'[5] Among the many examples that could be quoted are those of the Spanish ambassador in Paris, Bernardino de Mendoza, and the British minister in the Hague, Sir James Harris. In the 1580s, Mendoza bought secret information from Queen Elizabeth's ambassador in the French capital, Sir Edward Stafford, who had large gambling debts and a grudge against Sir Francis Walsingham (Box 1.1).[6] As for Harris, who was determined to win the struggle with the French for influence in the United Provinces in the mid-1780s, he ran a network of agents of the usual sort (which included minor Dutch politicians, the Sardinian consul in Amsterdam, and ship-watchers at Rotterdam) and drew even more heavily on secret service funds to subsidise those actively opposing the French party.

High-level informers would surely have had to be approached by the ambassador in person but in this twilight zone heads of mission had to be careful. After all, the efficient discharge of their other duties depended on the maintenance of satisfactory relations with their hosts, and this could clearly be risked by the exposure of

---

[3] Wicquefort and Callières, the two most impressive writers on diplomacy of the early modern period, both used this term with approval: Wicquefort, *The Embassador and His Functions*, p. 296. col. 2; Callières, *The Art of Diplomacy*, p. 80.

[4] As early as 1604, if not before, English ambassadors were being promised fixed allowances to cover this sort of thing, and by the middle of that century a 'Secret Service Fund' had been placed on a reasonably firm basis; beginning in 1797, there was an annual 'Secret Service Vote' in parliament. Although overall only a small proportion of this fund went to the ambassadors, the fund itself was large and in wartime the sums granted to a few of them could be very high indeed.

[5] Callières, *The Art of Diplomacy*, pp. 78–9; see also pp. 113–15.

[6] The only remaining question in this case is the *extent* to which Stafford was responsible for the damaging stream of intelligence obtained by Mendoza. This gave advance warning of the raid on Cadiz by English sea captain Sir Francis Drake, revealed instructions for the concentration of the English fleet, and provided much useful information on English diplomacy in Europe during the Anglo-Spanish war in 1587–8. Callières held up Spanish diplomacy as the model to emulate in this regard.

direct encouragement of treachery and other forms of espionage, not to mention covert action.[7] It was even riskier for a head of mission with the *formal* status of 'ambassador' – as opposed to one of lower grade or a mission secretary – because as courts became fussier about ceremonial and diplomatic missions became grander, the idea became fixed that the ambassador had the *full* representative character of his sovereign and thus always a formidable dignity to preserve. It is for these reasons that Abraham de Wicquefort, who was in a position to know (see Box 1.2), believed that diplomats of the 'second order' – who could move and mix more freely – were 'more proper to carry on an intrigue with safety.'[8]

Box 1.2 Abraham de Wicquefort

Abraham de Wicquefort (1598–1682) was an intelligencer, gazetteer and diplomat of the second rank. Born in Holland, nevertheless he served in Paris from 1626 until 1658 as Resident of the Elector of Brandenburg-Prussia, while selling intelligence and producing a weekly newsletter. Eventually falling foul of the French government, he was briefly imprisoned in the Bastille before being expelled. Thereafter, Wicquefort served the States General in his native Holland but – despite having taken an oath of secrecy – continued to sell intelligence to foreign powers, not least England, where the secretary of state's office composed instructions as to the intelligence it needed and received his coded despatches in reply. In 1675, Wicquefort was arrested by the Dutch for espionage and – despite his plea of diplomatic immunity on the grounds that he was concurrently the representative at The Hague of the Duke of Luneburg – convicted and sentenced to life imprisonment. In the prison of Loevestein (from which he escaped in 1679), he devoted his time to writing. The most important product of these years was his massive *L'Ambassadeur et Ses Fonctions*, which was written entirely from memory. First published in the year before he died and subsequently reissued many times, this became the greatest manual of diplomacy of the eighteenth century and is now regarded as the first substantial work to deal with what diplomats actually do as opposed to what they are supposed to do. It was ably translated into English in 1716 by John Digby as *The Embassador and His Functions*, and – since it is rare – I have published extracts from it in my *Diplomatic Classics*.

It is, therefore, not surprising that ambassadors were usually minded to detach themselves from direct dealings with the intelligencers and others in the lower ranks of the embassy's network. They did this, where possible, by delegating the responsibility to someone else in the embassy, although this was often difficult because until well into the nineteenth century the 'diplomatic' – as opposed to domestic – staff' of missions still consisted usually of no more than a secretary (possibly two) and some young men of his extended family or that of influential friends attached to the ambassador for the experience. Michel de Castelnau, the French Ambassador to England who was colluding with Mary Queen of Scots in the 1580s, was fortunate. His secretary of embassy, Nicolas

---

[7] Prior to going to Paris, Bernardino de Mendoza had been ambassador in London, and notoriously expelled for such activities.

[8] Wicquefort, *The Embassador and His Functions*, p. 34, col. 2.

Leclerc, seigneur de Courcelles, 'was not just a scribe: he had almost complete charge of Castelnau's operations concerning Mary and English Catholics, in which Castelnau wanted to be personally involved as little as possible,' writes John Bossy.[9] By contrast, in the Hague, two centuries later, Sir James Harris had 'to play a lone hand' because his own secretary of legation, William Gomm, although worthy, lacked the aptitude to be anything other than a scribe.[10] As a rule, nineteenth century ambassadors in the East did not have this problem (see Box 1.3).

> **Box 1.3 Gerald Fitzmaurice: 'The Wizard of Constantinople'**
> At embassies in the East, the task was usually transferred to a dragoman, an interpreter, information-gatherer and general 'fixer' in relations between the mission and the mysterious workings of the 'Oriental' bureaucracy. These were usually natives of the country concerned but during the course of the nineteenth century men of the ambassador's own nationality – believed to be more trustworthy – began to be employed in this role. In the British Embassy in Constantinople, the Armenian, Onik Effendi Parseghian, who was a key figure in the dragomanate but not officially recognized and paid from the mission's secret service fund, was a perfect example of the former; Gerald Fitzmaurice of the latter.
>   Fitzmaurice (1865–1939) was an unmarried Irish Catholic who spent his working life in the Levant Consular Service, rising in 1907 to one of its top posts: Chief Dragoman at the British embassy in Constantinople. Fitzmaurice was an outstanding example of a 'minister of the second order' – not just an intelligence-gatherer but also an intriguer, a man of action. He had made his name for 'special service' during the Armenian massacres in 1895–6 and then during the delimitation of the Aden frontier a decade later. Back in Abdul Hamid II's Constantinople, he became the British embassy's own spy master. He failed to anticipate the sudden Young Turks' revolution in 1908 but then made life difficult for them by encouraging their domestic opponents with advice, black propaganda and hints of British support. The counter-revolution of April 1909, in which he played such a strong hand, narrowly failed – but he remained at his post until shortly before the outbreak of war in 1914. It was he who was then attached to the British Legation at Sofia with a view to using this as a platform for a second attempt to overturn the then German-allied Turkish government and, failing that, to bribe the Bulgarians with an offer of £2.5m to attack the Turks and, by diverting them, guarantee the success of Britain's Dardanelles adventure. Neither of these long shots came off, and 'Fitzmaurice of Constantinople', as he was known in the Levant Service, or 'the Wizard of Constantinople' as he occasionally signed his private letters, ended up in London in Naval Intelligence, the division that not so long afterwards spawned Ian Fleming – and so 'James Bond'.

It was, as it happens, during the course of the nineteenth century that the attitude to secret intelligence of diplomatists as a body – not just those who were heads of mission – seems to have cooled further. This probably had much to do with the professionalization of diplomacy that was beginning to advance during these years, although it had been heralded as far back as the beginning of the eighteenth century in the establishment by the French foreign minister, Jean-Baptiste Colbert de Torcy, of a short-lived school for diplomats in Paris. The consequence was that those who entered

---

[9]   Unfortunately for the ambassador, Courcelles had been 'turned' by one of Walsingham's agents, Henry Fagot, who had succeeded in making himself a welcome member of the household – a penetration agent, Bossy, *Giordano Bruno and the Embassy Affair*, p. 20.

[10] Cobban, *Ambassadors and Secret Agents*, pp. 32–3.

diplomacy began to look on it less as a route into or temporary interlude in a political career, a means of making money quickly (if at Constantinople), or a way of combining public service with pursuit of a private enthusiasm such as archaeology that required long periods of absence abroad, but more as a life-long career.

Like all professions, diplomacy also acquired its attendant manuals for instruction and reference (see Box 1.2), including works of international law; and its sense of identity was reinforced by regular meetings of heads of mission in the diplomatic corps of each capital city for the purpose of discussing matters of common professional concern. The consequence was that a professional credo began to firm up, and central to this was the need for right behaviour. Without this there would be no trust, and without trust negotiations would be difficult and the credibility of information – even from friends – hard to judge. This prudential calculation was fortified not only by religion but also by the code of honour and social prejudices of the European aristocracy that was so strongly represented in the diplomatic service as well as the officer class. This was famously summed up early in the following century when, announcing the closure of the US State Department's Cipher Bureau, Secretary of State Henry Stimson remarked that 'Gentlemen do not read each others' mail.'[11] In any case, it was said, the practitioners of such dark arts were not only expensive and unreliable but also unnecessary; for an able professional diplomat who was liked and respected was perfectly capable of discovering all of the political secrets worth knowing by means of 'a good dinner and pleasant companionship', provided he exerted himself to mix widely and did not overlook the editors of leading newspapers. When secrets 'become serious,' wrote the British mid-Victorian journalist-diplomat, Eustace Clare Grenville-Murray, in his lively and acutely observed work on the profession, 'they become known.'[12] In sum, spies were lower class, untrustworthy, unsavoury in their methods – and dispensable.

From time to time, ambassadors still received and spent secret service money, some on bribery and influencing the press, but when Sir Ernest Satow published his own – and more famous – manual on diplomacy after the First World War, he was decidedly disapproving of bribery. While seeming to acknowledge the uncertainty on this subject of the 'law of nations' and that it was a 'more or less universal' means of obtaining secret information, Satow thought bribery immoral and only permissible as a last resort. More generally, he quoted Theodor Schmalz, one of two minor early nineteenth century German jurists upon whom he leaned heavily in this passage, that 'nothing is good politics but what is honourable' and that 'An uniform policy, armed with strength and

---

[11] Khazan, 'Gentlemen reading each others' mail'.
[12] Grenville-Murray, *Embassies and Foreign Courts*, pp. 260–1.

honesty, has little to apprehend from what is concealed, and steady attention to what passes around will mostly enable us to divine what is secret.'[13]

Sir Ernest Satow in 1903: British scholar-diplomat

Consuls as 'spies'

In the early modern period, consuls were merchants chosen from the ranks of a local trading settlement by the merchants themselves and, even after most were taken under the control of the state in later centuries, smoothing the path of commerce remained outwardly their sole responsibility. As a result, consular posts tended to be clustered mainly at major ports; but they were also to be found inland, and not just in major cities but also in provinces where there was interest in the popular mood or adjacent to frontiers of special concern. In many of these places, consuls were in practice encouraged by foreign ministries and war offices to gather and report political and military, as well as commercial intelligence.

---

[13] Satow, *A Guide to Diplomatic Practice*, pp. 142–4. It should, however, be added that Satow's German authorities were still of the view that the 'law of nations' was a system confined to Christian Europe, and that he probably believed that a less gentlemanly attitude to intelligence-gathering was more acceptable in the Orient, where his own long diplomatic career had been spent.

Box 1.4 A consular 'spy': George Stevens at Kherson
In the late 1850s and early 1860s, the British began to worry that Russia was re-building its Black Sea Fleet in violation of the treaty settling the recent Crimean War. As a result, one of the first things done by the then British consul-general at Odessa, E. C. Grenville-Murray, was to persuade the Foreign Office to give him a postage allowance for regular military intelligence reporting from the vice-consuls in his enormous district. Their response was lukewarm and the product was sparse but Grenville-Murray himself sent in a stream of reports and leaned for assistance on one vice-consul in particular, the truculent, Anglo-Levantine George Stevens. The latter's post, at Kherson, was the nearest to Nicolaieff (modern day Mikolaiv in Ukraine), which had major ship-building yards and was home to the Russian fleet. Stevens was ordered to report on developments at Nicolaieff, and on at least one occasion penetrated the dockyards in disguise. Unfortunately for Stevens, his consular 'cover' was transparent because there was no British commerce to protect at Kherson, and in 1865 he complained to the British ambassador at St. Petersburg that he had for seven years lived under suspicion of being a 'spy'.

Not all of them responded enthusiastically, especially when their 'cover' as commerce-preoccupied consul was thin (see Box 1.4) but some did, especially in war or near-war circumstances. An early instance is provided by Chasteau-Martin, who was consul to the English merchants at La Rochelle in the 1580s and therefore well placed to report on Spanish activities when Spain's threat to England was particularly acute. A key agent in Walsingham's network, he was paid a pension plus expenses and used these to place another agent in Madrid. Harris's reliance on a consul at Amsterdam two centuries later has already been mentioned. In the late nineteenth century and early twentieth, consuls also played a pivotal role in 'the Great Game': the intense secret intelligence competition for influence in the border regions between the British and Russian Empires in central and south Asia. The British sent 'military consuls' to posts close to Turkey's border with Russia, a very large network of agents was run by Patrick Stevens, British Consul at the Russian Black Sea port of Batum, and British and Russian consuls in Persia both ran their own agent networks. And in 1918, while the United States had no secret intelligence agencies, an American vice-consul, Robert Imbrie, set up and ran a short-lived network of agents from Petrograd, the aims of which were to gather intelligence both on the advancing German forces and the Bolsheviks. In peacetime, however, ambassadors and foreign ministries tended to be highly nervous about their consuls being engaged in secret intelligence work.

Main references and further reading

Spymasters

Adams, Simon; Bryson, Alan; Leimon, Mitchell, 'Walsingham, Sir Francis (c.1532–1590)', *ODNB* (2004)

Bemis, Samuel Flagg, 'British secret service and the French-American alliance', *The American Historical Review*, vol. 29 (3), April 1924

Budiansky, Stephen, *Her Majesty's Spymaster: Elizabeth I, Sir Francis Walsingham, and the Birth of Modern Espionage* (Viking: New York, 2005)

Croft, Pauline, 'Cecil, Robert, first earl of Salisbury (1563–1612)'. *ODNB* (2004)

Lee, Sidney, 'Walsingham, Francis (1530–1590)' *Dictionary of National Biography*, vol. 59; superseded generally by Adams *et al* above but has more on secret intelligence [www]

Szechi, Daniel (ed), *The Dangerous Trade: Spies, spymasters and the making of Europe* (Dundee University Press: Dundee, 2010)

Wikipedia (n.d.) 'Francis Walsingham'. This carefully written, authoritative and up-to-date piece [www]

Wilson, Derek, *Sir Francis Walsingham: A courtier in an age of terror* (Carroll & Graf: New York, 2007)

Ambassadors

Allen, E. John B., *Post and Courier Service in the Diplomacy of Early Modern Europe* (Martinus Nijhoff: The Hague, 1972)

Bossy, John, *Giordano Bruno and the Embassy Affair* (Vintage: London, 1991), Ch. 1

Callières, François de, *The Art of Diplomacy*, ed. H. M. A. Keens-Soper and Karl W. Schweizer (Leicester University Press and Holmes & Meier: New York 1983), Chs. 3 and 8 and App. 1 (Keens-Soper on 'The French Political Academy, 1712: A School for Ambassadors')

Cobban, Alfred, *Ambassadors and Secret Agents: The diplomacy of the First Earl of Malmesbury at The Hague* (Jonathan Cape: London, 1954)

Horn, D. B., *The British Diplomatic Service, 1689–1789* (Clarendon Press: Oxford, 1961), Ch. 14 ('Diplomatists and Secret Agents')

Hutchinson, Robert, *Elizabeth's Spy Master: Francis Walsingham and the secret war that saved England* (Phoenix: London, 2007)

Leimon, M. and G. Parker, 'Treason and plot in Elizabethan diplomacy: the "fame of Sir Edward Stafford" reconsidered', *English Historical Review*, 1996, vol. 111

McDermott, James, 'Stafford, Sir Edward (1552–1605)', *ODNB* (2012)

Middleton, C. R., *The Administration of British Foreign Policy, 1782–1846* (Duke University Press: Durham N.C., 1977), esp. App. VIII ('The Foreign Secret Service')

Potter, David (ed), *Foreign Intelligence and Information in Elizabethan England* (Cambridge University Press: Cambridge, 2004), Introduction

Read, Conyers, 'Walsingham and Burghley in Queen Elizabeth's Privy Council', *The English Historical Review*, vol. 28 (109), January 1913 [www]

Read, Conyers, *Mr Secretary Walsingham and the Policy of Queen Elizabeth* (Clarendon Press: Oxford, 1925)

Satow, Rt. Hon. Sir Ernest, *A Guide to Diplomatic Practice*, 2nd. rev. ed., vol. 1 (Longmans, Green: London, 1922), pp. 142–4 ('The use of Bribery')

Stone, Lawrence, *An Elizabethan: Sir Horatio Palavicino* (Clarendon Press: Oxford, 1956), Ch. 6 ('The Secret Agent')

Wicquefort, Abraham de, selections from, in Berridge, G. R. (ed), *Diplomatic Classics: Selected texts from Commynes to Vattel* (Palgrave Macmillan: Basingstoke, 2004), esp. pp. 125, 131

Consuls

Berridge, G. R., *Gerald Fitzmaurice (1865–1939): Chief Dragoman of the British Embassy in Turkey* (Martinus Nijhoff: Leiden and Boston, 2007), Chs. 2, 5, 6 and 9

Berridge, G. R., *Diplomacy, Satire, and the Victorians: The life and writings of E. C. Grenville-Murray*, 2nd ed, revised (DiploFoundation on ISSUU: Geneva and Malta, 2018), Ch. 3 (section 'Ordeal at Odessa')

Hughes, Michael, *Diplomacy before the Russian Revolution: Britain, Russia and the Old Diplomacy, 1894–1917* (Macmillan: Basingstoke, 2000), pp. 112–18 ('British consuls and the collection of secret intelligence')

Langbart, David A., 'Five Months in Petrograd in 1918: Robert W. Imbrie and the US Search for Information in Russia', *Studies in Intelligence* (CIA), vol. 52 (1), March 2008, Web Supplement, esp. Document II, in which the vice-consul (Imbrie) describes his agent network [www]

Lockhart, R. H. Bruce, *Memoirs of a British Agent* (Putnam: London and New York, 1932), Books II and III [www]

2   Arrival of the Secret Service

By the end of the nineteenth century, the ambassador had become a reluctant agent-runner. But while foreign ministries might have shared the diplomats' prejudices about secret intelligence personnel and methods, they were less inclined to agree that there was no need for them. Even in the deeply conservative higher commands of armies and navies the need for intelligence on potential enemies – if only for reliable maps of their coastlines and topography – began to be felt with gathering urgency. This was a consequence of developments that made strategic surprise a much greater risk, among them the electric telegraph, which made it possible to transmit military communications more quickly, and the advancing railway networks, which greatly increased the speed with which troops could be mobilized and deployed. The disasters suffered by the French army in the Franco-Prussian War in 1870–1 were only too clearly exacerbated by poor intelligence. It was, therefore, with a collective sigh of relief that, in response to this new situation, diplomats witnessed two innovations that promised to extend even further their arm's length relationship with the 'dirty' world of secret intelligence.

The first innovation was the regular appearance in the embassy of the military attaché, the herald of the military intelligence services; and the second was the emergence of the separate civilian foreign intelligence agency, or secret service, which in its bureaucratic permanence and formal detachment from policy-making was a creature 'far removed' from the spymaster system of earlier centuries.[14] This chapter will examine these changes, glance at the concept of the intelligence community, and reflect briefly on the significance for diplomacy of the secret political power of the secret service.

Military attachés

As early as 1680, the great scholar-diplomat Abraham de Wicquefort (Box 1.2) had shown concern at the tendency of some princes to require ambassadors to accompany them on military expeditions, since this implied that the ambassador's own prince endorsed the campaign, which might not have been the case. This would be avoided, he suggested, if embassies were to have a military officer attached to them, for he would not only be a natural substitute for the ambassador but also be more 'capable of judging of martial actions.'[15]

---

[14]   Herman, *Intelligence Power in Peace and War*, p. 34.

[15]   Wicquefort, *The Embassador and His Functions*, p. 297, col. 2.

Foreign military attachés with their German escorts at the Imperial manoeuvres, 1904

Whether in part for this reason or not, by the end of the eighteenth century army and navy officers began occasionally to make casual appearances in embassies. But it was not until the following century that it became a reflex of the major states formally to provide embassies with military attachés. (Naval and then air attachés were later added and came to be known collectively as service or defense attachés.) Occasionally, too, they were to be found in consulates, including those close to a major naval base such as Kronstadt, the Russian base at the head of the Gulf of Finland.

The military attaché was the most visible and often probably the most important figure in the new military intelligence services (see below) but preceded their appearance by some decades. There were General Staff officers in Prussia's main embassies as early as 1817, military attachés in French embassies from the 1830s, and by the second half of the century they were a regular feature of diplomatic life. In the course of the twentieth century, service attachés became as common in peacetime as in war, although numerous side accreditations were frequent.

The minimum duties of service attachés (who sometimes recruit their own agents) include obtaining intelligence on the armed forces of the country or countries to which they are accredited: the size and equipment of the armed forces in particular but also their morale, training, geographical disposition, tactical and strategic doctrines, defensive fortifications, capacity for swift mobilization, and so on. Service attachés are well placed to do this because it became customary for them to be closely involved in defence collaboration when relations were friendly, and – whether they were or not – to enjoy the hard-drinking intimacy of their 'comrades in arms' at the post to which they were accredited, for eventually these tended to form a well-organized and often convivial sub-division of the diplomatic corps, with its own doyen.

It came to be well understood that the exchange of service attachés, by reducing mutual suspicions, contributes to the stability of the balance of power. Even during tense passages of the Cold War they were tolerated by both sides. However, because of the enduring suspicion of them as 'military spies', the Vienna Convention on Diplomatic Relations 1961 (VCDR) stipulates in article 7 that, apart from the head of mission (for whom agrément is mandatory), the service attaché is the only member of the staff of a diplomatic mission whose name might, if the receiving state so requires, need to be submitted for approval prior to appointment. In practice, this is something on which receiving states have usually insisted.

The introduction of service attachés has certainly relieved diplomats of responsibility for the gathering of military intelligence, while their vetting by receiving states has gone some way to reduce the anxiety of ambassadors that the officers appointed are of the sort likely to make trouble. Nevertheless, service attachés have sometimes proved to be a mixed blessing. This is because their primary allegiance is to armed forces' intelligence headquarters at home or to a defence ministry; because they are inclined to adjust imperfectly to the atmosphere and routines of an embassy; and because when a mission's defence section is large it is not unusual to find it housed separately from the building containing the chancery. The consequence of these circumstances is that service attachés are sometimes required by their military masters to engage in activities that are illegal or borderline illegal, and in carrying them out might be insensitive to the embarrassment they are likely to cause a head of mission. This can make for uncomfortable relations in a peacetime mission, and worse relations still if the military establishment and the foreign ministry are tugging in different directions on policy towards the state where the embassy is based. On the other hand, it is true that embarrassing incidents tend soon to be forgotten. For example, improving relations between Israel and Russia suffered nothing more than a temporary hiccup following the expulsion from Moscow in May 2011 of the Israeli military attaché on grounds of espionage. As often as not, too, such expulsions are a symptom rather than a cause of bad relations, as when Venezuela gave two US defense attachés 24 hours to get out of Caracas in March 2013.

Defence intelligence services

Since the avoidance of strategic surprise is usually the top priority of foreign intelligence-gathering, its bureaucratization in the late nineteenth and early twentieth centuries was led by the military; that is, by army high commands and ministries of war. By this time, bureaucracy – pursuit of an objective with the aid of an impersonal, complex administrative machine – was already emerging as a distinguishing feature of the activities of the modern state, as noted with qualified praise by the German sociologist Max Weber. And for intelligence-gathering, it had at least two advantages. First, it facilitated the storage, retrieval, analysis, and distribution through government of the increasing flow of information that was arriving. Second, it made it possible to build up files on individual agents which contained not only their safe contact details but also their track records of providing reliable information, thereby reducing the risk of paying out large sums to rogues.

Box 2.1 Prussian/German military intelligence

To its twentieth century enemies, the Prussian/German General Staff, which originated in a reorganization of 1803, was the epitome of professional militarism and thus an object of fear and disgust. But it was much admired in the nineteenth century, for it gave form to the idea that military commanders should be required to take the advice of an elite of highly educated and broadly trained officers selected on merit rather than social class; General Carl von Clausewitz, author of the classic work, *Vom Kriege* [*On War*], was one of its earliest members. The General Staff was initially subordinate to the Ministry of War but such was the growth in its prestige that in 1883 it achieved complete independence. Its main budget funded three divisions charged with investigating all matters of military interest in foreign countries, the first being responsible for Sweden, Norway, Turkey and Austria; the second for Germany, Italy and Switzerland; and the third for France, England, Belgium, the Netherlands, Spain, Portugal and America. A fourth division was responsible for military railway transport, while an additional budget provided, among other things, for a war history department and geographical-statistical studies.

Under the Versailles Treaty ending the First World War, defeated Germany was forbidden a General Staff and associated military intelligence service. But the service re-emerged in 1920–1 as the Abwehr, a small section under the Ministry of Defence. 'Abwehr' is the German word for 'fending off' or 'defence' (in this context signifying 'counter-espionage'), and the name was employed to reassure the inter-allied commission that the purpose of the revived service was nothing to be worried about. The Abwehr gradually became a full military intelligence service, especially after the Nazi Party came to power in Germany in 1933 but was generally ineffective. It was also anti-Nazi, and its last chief prior to its merger in 1944 with the notorious SS was Admiral Canaris, who was executed for treason in April 1945. After the war, the residue of German intelligence officers (the Gehlen Organization) was taken under the wing of the CIA, until in 1956 the Bundesnachrichtendienst (Federal Intelligence Service) was formed. The BND gives Germany one agency for both military and civil (political and economic) intelligence.

Notable examples of the nascent defence intelligence services are provided by the intelligence divisions of the Prussian General Staff (Box 2.1) and the services of France and Britain which Prussia's initial achievements helped to inspire.

Admiral Wilhelm Canaris: head of the Abwehr, 1940

However, the Prussians apart, military leadership of the bureaucratization of secret intelligence did not move quickly because military establishments everywhere were highly conservative institutions. In France, foreign intelligence – as opposed to domestic surveillance – was not put on a permanent basis until the Section de Statistiques et de Reconnaissances of the Deuxième Bureau of the General Staff was created in 1871. And in Britain, while military intelligence was established in the War Office during the Crimean War, it did little beyond map-making until the 1870s, and it was 1877 before the Naval Intelligence Department appeared. The process of bureaucratization was consolidated only by the emergency of the First World War. When this was over, it was the threat of 'capitalist encirclement' that gave impetus to the organization of military intelligence in the new Soviet Union; hence the Glavnoye Razvedyvatelnoye Upravleniye (GRU), which is still active today.

Civilian intelligence services

The bureaucratization of military intelligence might have come first but the improvements that came with it were sometimes more appreciated by foreign ministries than the military themselves. Foreign ministries were also keen to secure their own secret services because of the reluctance or inability of military intelligence to seek *political* information; also because, naturally enough, foreign ministries tended to regard foreign affairs as their special preserve. Thus, despite the prestige of the General Staff, the German foreign ministry established a political foreign intelligence service during the First World War. In Britain, the Secret Intelligence Service (SIS) (Box 2.2) and signals intelligence (given its present name Government Communications Headquarters,

GCHQ, in 1942) fell under Foreign Office control after that conflict, and have remained responsible to it ever since. Other civilian intelligence services achieved more independence; notable among these is the American Central Intelligence Agency (CIA) established in 1947, which – like SIS – had its roots in military intelligence, the wartime Office of Strategic Services (OSS).

Box 2.2 The British Secret Intelligence Service (SIS)

Also known as MI6, the cover name given to it in the Second World War, SIS began life as the foreign department of the Secret Service Bureau established in 1909 in response to alarm at the possibility of a German invasion. (The Bureau's home department was responsible for counter-espionage and was the forerunner of today's Security Service, also known as MI5.) Its first head was a naval captain, Mansfield Cumming ('C'), and it was initially answerable to the Admiralty. Since Cumming's time, the head of SIS has always been known as 'C' and the service sometimes referred to simply as 'C's organization'.

Sir Mansfield Cumming: first head of SIS

The full-time members of such services, 'intelligence officers' as opposed to 'spies' or 'agents', work in the guise of diplomats or consular officers but under their own names. They are, therefore, sometimes described as 'legals'. A much smaller number of intelligence officers are 'illegals' or 'NOCs' (non-official cover). (Legals and illegals are both discussed in the next chapter.)

Operations conducted by a secret service designed to support friends and eliminate enemies abroad sometimes involve violence but more often money, supplies and propaganda. Most secret services engage in this sort of thing from time to time, although some rather more than others. The GRU has a particularly bad reputation for this because of the clumsy attempt by two of its officers to murder a Russian defector, Sergei Skripal, with the nerve agent Novichok in the United Kingdom in March

2018. But during the Cold War, the CIA became legendary for its own covert actions, especially in Central and South America, and – via its Counterterrorism Centre Special Operations branch – revived this reputation, particularly in Afghanistan and Pakistan, during the so-called 'War on Terror'. Among other secret services with reputations for no-holds-barred political warfare are Israel's Mossad and the secret services of France. In 1985, French intelligence officers blew up and sank in a New Zealand harbour the Greenpeace vessel, *Rainbow Warrior*, which was planning to inconvenience French nuclear testing on Moruroa atoll. For reasons that will be obvious, it is a common view in the secret world that covert action has its role, but that covert action and intelligence-gathering should not be handled by the same agency.

The intelligence community

Major powers and middle powers have often had two and sometimes many more secret intelligence agencies, some answering only to the head of government or executive president (as in the USA) and others to different state ministries. In the United States, six separate departments run intelligence services: Defense, Energy, Homeland Security, Justice, State. and Treasury. Moreover, middle powers do not necessarily have fewer agencies (loosely defined) than major powers. Pakistan, for example, has nine intelligence agencies, which is about the same as the United Kingdom.

It is not necessarily a bad thing to have numerous agencies with some overlapping responsibilities, for this reduces the likelihood that an intelligence assessment will go untested and diminishes the risk that one agency will become politically too powerful. What is usefully termed 'tailored intelligence' – giving 'customers' a dedicated agency of their own people (for example, naval intelligence for the navy) – also 'improves communication and trust between them.'[16] But the rivalries between such agencies, which are notorious, can be debilitating, particularly when this results in confusion over responsibility or refusal to share intelligence. The bureaucratization of secret intelligence would not, therefore, have been complete without a move to produce a rational administrative structure that allocated priorities to and harmonised the relations between them, and also distilled their product for the benefit of their busy political masters. Hence the 'intelligence community' – more than an aspirational name, if in practice less than the label implies.

Box 2.3 The 'Elements' of the US Intelligence Community
(1) Office of the Director of National Intelligence (2) Central Intelligence Agency (3) Department of Defense – National Security Agency (4) Department of Defense – Defense Intelligence Agency (5) Department of Justice – FBI (6) Department of State – Intelligence and Research Bureau (7) Department of Homeland Security – Office of Intelligence and Analysis (8) Department of Justice –

---

16 National Research Council, *Intelligence Analysis for Tomorrow*, p. 8.

Drug Enforcement Administration, Office of National Security Intelligence (9) Department of the Treasury – Office of Intelligence and Analysis (10) Department of Energy – Office of Intelligence and Counterintelligence (11) Department of Defense – National Geospatial-Intelligence Agency (12) Department of Defense – National Reconnaissance Office (13) Air Force Intelligence, Surveillance and Reconnaissance (14) Army Military Intelligence (15) US Navy – Office of Naval Intelligence (16) Marine Corps Intelligence (17) Department of Homeland Security – Coast Guard Intelligence. Source: Devine and Peters, 'U.S. Intelligence Community Elements'.

The paradigm case of an intelligence community is that of the United States, which was created by statute in 1992. At the time of writing this formally contains 17 'elements' (Box 2.3), as they are officially described in a further attempt to change the agencies' mind sets: to encourage them to think of themselves less as independent bodies and more as essential components of a complex, well-integrated whole. The US intelligence community also has a simple hierarchy in that the first element – the Director of National Intelligence (DNI) – is, as the name implies, the head of the entire body.[17] This office, although long mooted, was created only in 2005, following the conclusion that poor information-sharing and general lack of coordination between different agencies had contributed to the success of the 9/11 attacks on the USA in 2001 and the false belief in 2003 that Iraq had WMD. The DNI, assisted by the National Intelligence Council, oversees and directs implementation of the National Intelligence Program and 'acts as the principal advisor to the President, the National Security Council, and the Homeland Security Council for intelligence matters related to national security.'[18] A top priority of the Office of the DNI is to erode the traditional 'need-to-know' culture of the secret intelligence world and instead promote information sharing.

Secret intelligence as secret power

The risk of secret security and intelligence agencies wielding secret power in the state makes their control an important concern for government in general and – because, as we shall see, they live so closely with them – for diplomats in particular. US president Donald Trump, who periodically complains about the manoeuvrings against him of the 'deep state' and has expressed particular distrust of the CIA and the FBI, is not the first political leader to give voice to views of this sort. An obvious reason for this is that, broadly defined, intelligence communities have domestic as well as foreign responsibilities. Another is their modus operandi, which includes skill in political warfare and control of extensive secret funds. In some states, secret intelligence agencies make a great deal of extra money through criminal activities such as drug-trafficking, a credible charge frequently levelled at Pakistan's Inter-Services Intelligence (ISI), a

---

[17]   The British equivalent is the Joint Intelligence Organization.
[18]   Office of the DNI [www]

notorious 'state within a state'. In addition, their knowledge of 'where the bodies are buried', whether metaphorically or, in the case of Saudi Arabia, in reality, always has the potential to give them leverage over a political leader – provided that leader is capable of embarrassment. Finally, like most institutions, secret services tend to have deep-rooted political prejudices that might periodically be at odds with the governments they serve. For example, in France the Deuxième Bureau was notoriously anti-semitic, while later the SDECE had a strong pro-colonialists bias; in Germany, as we have already seen, the Abwehr was hostile to its Nazi masters (Box 2.1); and, with its deep attachment to Communism, in 1991 the KGB came close to overthrowing the reformist Soviet leader, Mikhail Gorbachev.

Formally, as already noted, the agencies are answerable either directly to the head of government or a ministry. In the first case, they are sometimes said to be 'independent' but this only means that they are independent of any ministry; in effect, therefore, they are ministries in their own right. Examples include the CIA, the BND (Box 2.1), Mossad (Israel), the SVR (Russia), and – making the point rather neatly – the Chinese *Ministry* of State Security. Effective executive oversight of the secret intelligence agencies, meaning well-informed, general direction of their work, is the most potent form of control, and in the liberal-democracies, including those in the post-Communist states, there is now much greater sensitivity to the means by which this should be achieved. But if the executive itself is weak, vicious, or corrupt, what else can be done? One possible solution is to try a different *form* of executive oversight. For example, after the Second World War the French intelligence service, SDECE – today the Direction Générale de la Sécurité Extérieure (DGSE) – reported directly to the prime minister but, following numerous scandals, in 1962 it was placed by President De Gaulle under the Ministry of Defence. Another answer, and now much more common solution, is to subject the secret agencies to oversight by a bipartisan select committee of members of an elected assembly. The lead in such 'parliamentary oversight' was taken by the US Congress in the mid-1970s, following domestic spying scandals and revelations concerning CIA covert operations, and by 2006 had become 'the norm in democratic states.'[19]

Box 2.4 Congressional oversight of the US Intelligence Community
Both houses of Congress have a select committee on intelligence. Since they control the funding of the Intelligence Community (Box 2.3), initiate legislation affecting it, have subpoena powers, and are supported by weighty staffs, considerable influence backs up their oversight responsibilities. The Senate Select Committee on Intelligence, which was created in 1976, has 15 members: eight senators from the majority party (one of whom has the chair) and seven from the minority, irrespective of the

---

[19] Born and Leigh, 'Democratic accountability of intelligence services', p. 2. On its problems, see pp. 10–13 of same reference and Caparini, M., 'Controlling and overseeing intelligence services in democratic states', pp. 13–14.

fluctuating representation of the parties in the Senate as a whole. It meets frequently, usually in closed session. The House 'Permanent Select Committee on Intelligence' (so-called to distinguish it from the temporary creation of the previous two years and now commonly known as the 'House Intelligence Committee') was created in 1977. House rules are silent on the size and party ratios of this committee, as on almost all other House committees, with two consequences: first, they are usually determined by negotiation between the majority and minority leaderships; second, the majority party in the House has a more favourable proportion of committee members than it has of congressmen in the House as a whole. Since the early 1980s, the majority party on the House Intelligence Committee has had on average three more members than the minority party, one of whom holds the chair. At the time of writing (December 2018) the Republicans have thirteen seats and the Democrats have nine but this is set to be reversed following the Democrat gains in the House in the mid-term elections. The rules of procedure of the Senate Select Committee on Intelligence can be seen on its website. See also Glassman and Eckman, 'House Committee party ratios'; Johnson *et al*, *House Practice*, pp. 248–9.

The provisions for greater accountability will have provided some reassurance to the diplomats of the liberal-democracies that the intelligence officers with whom they work closely are not going to embarrass them. On the other hand, because few of these committees have oversight of operational matters – as opposed to policy, administration and expenditure – they 'can have or give no assurance about the efficiency or the legality of the intelligence services.'[20] Besides, the number of liberal-democracies (always a minority) is shrinking.[21]

Main references and further reading

Andrew, Christopher and David Dilks (eds.), *The Missing Dimension: Governments and intelligence communities in the twentieth century* (Macmillan: London, 1984)

Champion, Brian, 'Spies (look) like us: the early use of business and civilian covers in covert operations', *International Journal of Intelligence and Counter-Intelligence*, vol. 21 (3), 2008

Herman, Michael, *Intelligence Power in Peace and War* (Cambridge University Press and the Royal Institute of International Affairs: Cambridge, 1996), Chs. 1 and 2

Richter, L., 'Military and Civil Intelligence Services in Germany from World War I to the end of the Weimar Republic' in H. Bungert, J. G. Heitmann and Michael Wala (eds) *Secret Intelligence in the Twentieth Century* (Cass: London, 2003)

Spy Museum [Washington DC] (n.d.) 'Language of Espionage' [www]

Military

Alexander, Martin, 'Did the Deuxième Bureau work? The role of intelligence in French defence policy and strategy, 1919–39'. *Intelligence and National Security*, vol. 6 (2), 1991

BBC News, 'Pakistan's shadowy secret service, the ISI', 3 May 2011 [www]

Berridge, G. R., *Embassies in Armed Conflict* (Continuum: New York and London, 2012), Chs. 1 and 4 (section 'Espionage and special operations')

Berridge, G. R. and Lorna Lloyd, *The Palgrave Macmillan Dictionary of Diplomacy* (Palgrave Macmillan: Basingstoke, 2012) – on the numerous variations on the term 'military attaché'.

---

[20] Born and Leigh, 'Democratic accountability of intelligence services', p. 12. The American select committees are exceptional in their oversight of operations. The British 'Intelligence and Security Committee of Parliament' had such oversight nominally added to its own functions in 2013 but on such restrictive conditions as to make it of little value, Justice and Security Act, 2013, Part 1, Sec. 2 (3) [www]

[21] See The Economist Intelligence Unit, 'Democracy Index 2017: Free speech under attack'[www]

Millotat, C. O. E., 'Understanding the Prussian-German General Staff system' (Strategic Studies Institute: U.S. Army War College, 20 March 1992), Ch. 3 [www]

Seligman, M. S., *Spies in Uniform: British military and naval intelligence on the eve of the First World War* (Oxford University Press: Oxford, 2006), Chs. 2 and 3

Civilian

Andrew, Christopher and Oleg Gordievsky (eds.), *Instructions from the Centre: Top Secret Files on KGB Foreign Operations, 1975–85* (Hodder and Stoughton: London, 1991); published by Stanford UP in 1993 as *Comrade Kryuchkov's Instructions*

Andrew, C., and V. Mitrokhin, *The Mitrokhin Archive: The KGB in Europe and the West* (Penguin: London and New York, 1999). A work of exceptional interest and importance; extremely long and detailed; a book to be dipped into.

Bower, Tom, *The Perfect English Spy: Sir Dick White and the secret war, 1935–90* (Heinemann: London, 1995)

Chesterman, S., 'The spy who came in from the Cold War: intelligence and international law', *Michigan Journal of International Law*, 2005–6, vol. 27 [www]

Corera, Gordon, *MI6: Life and death in the British Secret Service* (Weidenfeld and Nicolson: London, 2011)

Dulles, Allen, *The Craft of Intelligence* (Signet: New York, 1965)

Jeffery, Keith, *MI6: The history of the Secret Intelligence Service, 1909–1949* (Bloomsbury: London, 2010). The official history. Long on detail.

Judd, Alan. *The Quest for C: Sir Mansfield Cumming and the founding of the British Secret Service* (HarperCollins: London, 1999)

Macintyre, Ben, *The Spy and the Traitor: The greatest espionage story of the Cold War* (Viking: London, 2018)

Porch, D., *The French Secret Services: From the Dreyfus Affair to the Gulf War* (Macmillan: London and Basingstoke, 1996), Chs. 1 and 2

Sisman, Adam, *John le Carré: The biography* (Bloomsbury: London, 2015)

Tenet, G., *At the Center of the Storm: My years at the CIA* (HarperCollins: New York, 2007), Chs. 12 and 13

There is a useful review of '8 books about the CIA' by Katherine Whittemore in *The Boston Globe*, 4 August 2012 [www]

The intelligence community

Andrew, C., *Secret Service: The making of the British intelligence community* (Heinemann: London, 1985), Chs. 1–4

DeVine, Michael E. and Heidi M. Peters, 'U.S. Intelligence Community Elements: Establishment provisions', *Congressional Research Service*, 27 June 2018 [www]

FAS, *The Evolution of the U.S. Intelligence Community – An Historical Overview*, 1996 [www]

FAS (n.d.), 'Pakistan Intelligence Agencies' [www]

Richelson, Jeffrey T., *The US Intelligence Community*, 7th edn (Westview Press: Boulder, Colo., 2015)

U.S. Intelligence Community, *Information Sharing Strategy* (2008) [www]

U.S. Intelligence Community, *Strategic Intent for Information Sharing, 2011–2015* (2011) [www]

Secret intelligence as secret power

Baldino, D., *Democratic Oversight of Intelligence Services* (Federation Press: Leichhardt, Australia, 2010)

Born, Hans and Ian Leigh, 'Democratic accountability of intelligence services', *Policy Paper 19* (Geneva Centre for the Democratic Control of Armed Forces, 2007). Succinct and authoritative but now a little dated [www]

Caparini, M., 'Controlling and overseeing intelligence services in democratic states', in Caparini, M. and H. Born (eds.), *Democratic Control of Intelligence Services: Containing rogue elephants* (Routledge: London, 2007)

3   Cuckoos in the Nest?

In 1883 the Czarist secret police, the Okhrana, installed the headquarters of its Foreign Bureau in the consular section of the Russian Embassy in Paris, from which it liaised with *agenturas* in Berlin, Sofia and elsewhere. And in 1919, the British Secret Intelligence Service secured the reluctant agreement of the Foreign Office to give its officers cover as vice-consuls with responsibility for passport control work (Box 3.1). But it was not until after the Second World War, by which time secret services were more well established, that it became the norm for states to give legal cover in diplomatic and consular missions to the greater proportion of their intelligence officers abroad; such cover is now also provided by appointments in permanent missions and secretariats attached to international organizations such as the United Nations. Large numbers of intelligence officers still populate diplomatic missions despite the serious threat posed to Humint by the dramatic advances made in the technical means of intelligence-gathering since the middle of the last century. For example, if MI5 had correctly identified them, there were at least 23 'undeclared' intelligence officers in the Russian Embassy in London in March 2018 because this was the number expelled in response to the Skripal poisoning.

> **Box 3.1 SIS and Passport Control Officer cover**
> Prior to the Second World War, the Foreign Office refused to give SIS officers any cover in its overseas posts other than that of Passport Control Officer (PCO). But in addition to the disguise provided, the position had two other advantages: first, it gave immediate access to information on individuals of interest passing through border controls; and second, the pay for the work provided a useful supplement to the parliament-voted Secret Service budget. The trouble was that it tied SIS representation to those countries with which the UK had visa agreements and, because the cover was restricted to one position only, it soon became widely known that all PCOs were in reality SIS officers. This being the case, concluded an official report in 1944, 'little extra harm would have been done by affixing a brass plate "British Secret Service" to the door of their office.' Despite this, when the US State Department agreed in 1946 to give diplomatic cover to operatives of the new Central Intelligence Group (later CIA), it 'sugar coated' the news for chiefs of mission by emphasising not only that the intelligence officers would answer to them but also be concerned chiefly with 'security intelligence' or helping missions by undertaking the clerical work of file-checks on applicants for visas and passports. Either because old habits die hard or because it was thought to be a clever double bluff, when Ruari Chisholm was made chief of the SIS station in the British embassy in Moscow in 1960 he was given cover as '2nd Secretary (Head of Visa Section)'.

It was certainly technical means – typified by the spy satellite – that was the main reason for the cloud hovering over Humint at the end of the last century but it was not helped by the reputation it had acquired with 'users' for providing information that was not only – in modern conditions – too slow to dig out and deliver but also difficult to judge for reliability when it arrived. On the other hand, aside from the fact that most

SOVIET UNION.		
Moscow	Ambassador	Sir Frank Roberts, K.C.M.G.
	Minister	W. Barker, C.M.G., O.B.E.
	1st Secretary	K. R. Oakeshott.
	Counsellor (Commercial) ...	H. W. King, M.B.E.
	1st Secretary (Commercial) ...	K. J. Uffen.
	3rd Secretary (Commercial) ...	L. E. Sturmey.
	1st Secretary and Cultural Attaché ...	C. M. James.
	2nd Secretary	M. J. E. Fretwell.
	,, ,, ...	T. N. Haining.
	,, ,, ...	S. W. Martin.
	3rd Secretary	D. C. Thomas.
	1st Secretary and Head of Russian Secretariat	C. R. A. Rae.
	2nd Secretary	M. J. F. Duncan.
	,, ,, ...	R. A. Longmire.
	3rd Secretary	G. D. G. Murrell.
	2nd Secretary (Head of Visa Section)	R. W. Chisholm.
	Junior Attaché	Miss P. Fletcher.
	,, ,, ...	Miss J. M. King.
	Naval Attaché	Capt. J. F. R. Dreyer, R.N.
	Assistant Naval Attaché ...	Lt. Cdr. H. M. Ellis, R.N.
	,, ,, ,, ...	Lt.-Cdr. J. L. Varley, R.N.
	Military Attaché	Brigadier I. R. Burrows, O.E
	Assistant Military Attaché (Technical)	Major J. L. Jealous.
	Air Attaché	Gp. Capt. M. D. Lyne.
	Assistant Air Attaché	Fl.-Lt. R. McQ. Davies.
	,, ,, ,, (Technical) ...	Sq. Ldr. N. J. Gardner.
	Scientific Attaché	D. A. Senior.
	Honorary Chaplain	Rev. J. B. Roberts.
	1st Secretary and Embassy Medical Officer	Dr. T. R. Austin.
	1st Secretary, Administration Officer and Consul (s)	A. J. V. George.
	2nd Secretary	M. Millar.
	3rd Secretary	C. G. F. James, M.B.E.
	,, ,, ...	J. R. Neaves.
	Junior Attaché	W. E. Downing.
	,, ,, ...	A. Riches.
	,, ,, ...	G. P. Lockton.

Staff of British Embassy Moscow, Foreign Office List 1961

states either cannot afford or do not have access to the product of advanced technical means of intelligence-gathering, their limitations were highlighted by the failure to understand in 2003 that Saddam Hussein's Iraq did not possess WMD. Technical means cannot hear or see everything; nor cultivate agents of influence; nor – drone strikes apart – carry out more aggressive special operations in the absence of a major contribution by field officers and their agents. This has led to a reappraisal of Humint, which, as well as being cheap compared to other methods of collection, has 'special advantages' of its own. Notable among these are an unrivalled ability to penetrate terrorist groups, procure top secret state documents and also assist Sigint itself; for example, by planting bugging

The Common Cuckoo

devices and inserting infected flash drives into air-gapped computers or closed computer networks. Humint is, then, still important, and diplomatic cover for its officers is still popular. But why should such cover remain the disguise of choice? How does it work? And – as is sometimes grumbled by ambassadors – do intelligence officers in embassy nests really resemble cuckoos, those parasitic bullies of the bird world?

The advantages of diplomatic cover

Diplomatic cover has at least four advantages for intelligence officers.

First, it is a good disguise because intelligence officers not only tend to come from the same backgrounds as diplomats but also do much the same sort of thing. Real diplomats also seek information and cultivate friends in high places.

Second, the known presence of intelligence officers in embassies makes these missions magnets for those with secrets to divulge, whether they choose to do this by discreet signalling or openly walking through their doors. Swift assessments of the potential value and credibility of agents recruited in this way can be made and their exfiltration assisted should it become necessary. 'Walk-ins' are sometimes the most valuable of sources although usually difficult to distinguish from deliberate fakes ('dangles'). One of the most remarkable among the genuine sort was the KGB archivist Vasili Mitrokhin, who walked into the British embassy in Latvia in early 1992 and, after several return journeys to Moscow, was successfully exfiltrated by SIS – together with the massive archive on which this chapter draws heavily – later in the year. Seven years earlier, KGB colonel Oleg Gordievsky, another defector of enormous value to the West, whose intelligence while still an agent in place on the unfounded Soviet fear of American preparations for a pre-emptive nuclear first strike had greatly helped to avoid a catastrophic war in 1983, had been successfully exfiltrated by the SIS station in the British Embassy in Moscow.[22] Also worth mentioning are Ashraf Marwan, the highly placed Egyptian whose career as a Mossad agent began with an approach to the Israeli embassy in London in 1970; and Aldrich Ames, the CIA officer whose own double life commenced when he entered the Soviet embassy in Washington in 1985.

---

[22] Gordievsky was not a walk-in but had been delicately courted by the SIS station in the British embassy in Copenhagen following his posting to the Danish capital in 1972.

The third and most important advantage of diplomatic cover is the security it gives to intelligence officers. With diplomatic status, they have all of the privileges and immunities of genuine diplomats, whether inside or outside the embassy's walls. The worst that can befall them is to be PNG-d. By contrast, 'illegals' or – in American usage, NOCs (Non-Official Cover) – have no immunity and, if caught, usually face long-term prison sentences, or worse.

Box 3.2 The CIA's failed bid for more NOCs

Beginning in the mid-1950s, the CIA made efforts to halt the trend to more use of official cover, even setting as a long term goal having more NOCs than officers working legally in embassies. This was prompted partly by reductions in the opportunities for official cover caused by periodic economies in the number of US officials and installations overseas and partly by evidence that diplomatic cover was beginning to provide insufficient protection to officers in turbulent regions. It turned out to be wishful thinking not only because recruiting, training and setting up suitable candidates for NOC work was immensely difficult and took years but also because the constant demand of official customers was for delivery of sound intelligence 'now'. This story leaps out of the pages of the 659 CIA documents brought up by a search for "official cover" using CREST (CIA Records Search Tool). In addition, in states where counter-intelligence was highly efficient, as in the Soviet Union, the likely arrest of CIA officers without diplomatic immunity would also have served merely to provide the local authority with 'trade bait' – prisoners to be used in swap negotiations.

Furthermore, much time and trouble is required to provide them with the kind of 'legend' that will withstand scrutiny, and their numbers are consequently small (Box 3.2).

US Embassy compound in Somalia, evacuated 1991

Diplomatic status also gives intelligence officers, together with their work stations and accommodation, the physical protection afforded by the walled compounds in which many embassies and staff living quarters are now located in conflict zones. The importance of such protection has also increased further in recent years: first, because the multiplication of threats has led to the hurried expansion of many intelligence agencies, with the consequent need to send untested officers into dangerous operational environments; and second, because 'digital exhaust' fumes now make it so much easier to identify and expose intelligence officers.[23]

Finally, it is important to add that Sigint officers and technicians, as well as Humint officers, benefit from being hidden in diplomatic or consular premises. This is because of the customary proximity of embassies to government buildings, and the occasional nearness of consulates to sites of scientific and technical interest (Box 3.3). However, the increased use of fibre-optic cables for international communications, coupled with the recent use of aerial platforms for Sigint operations, is probably reducing the value of the embassies of the major powers for eavesdropping purposes.

Box 3.3 Sigint bases in Soviet diplomatic and consular posts in the Cold War

During the Cold War, the GRU and the KGB both developed massive Sigint networks based largely in Soviet embassies and consulates, especially in the USA. In 1963 the KGB established a radio intercept post at the Soviet embassy in Mexico City and more valuable ones swiftly followed – on the top floor of the Washington embassy (only three blocks from the White House) in 1966 and in the New York consulate-general in the year after. By the 1970s, the KGB had five separate intercept posts at different diplomatic facilities in the Washington area and four in the greater New York City region, including one at the 'diplomatic *dacha*' in Glen Cove, Long Island. Since the KGB lacked high-level penetration agents in Washington during these years, these Sigint posts were then its chief sources of intelligence on US foreign and defence policy and in general were probably a good thing because they made it difficult for Moscow to sustain its long-held belief that America was planning a nuclear first strike. In 1976 an intercept post was also established in the KGB residency in the tall building occupied by the Soviet consulate-general in San Francisco, which became a perfect hub for eavesdropping on Silicon Valley until closed down on American insistence in August 2017.

By the early1980s, the KGB had Sigint stations in 34 diplomatic or consular posts in 27 states. Astonishingly enough, the GRU's network of diplomatic listening posts (which included Soviet trade missions) was by then even bigger than this. The expansion continued remorselessly, so that by 1989 the KGB and the GRU were operating – often competitively – covert listening posts in 62 countries.

Embassy 'stations'

Within the embassies and more important consular posts of larger states, intelligence officers – like other specialist attachés – are to be found organized in sections. The CIA, SIS, Mossad and others refer to these as 'stations' while the Russian agencies call them 'residencies' (*rezidentury*). Such sections are formally subordinate to the ambassador

---

23 Corera, 'The spies of tomorrow'. Had he written this piece after the Skripal affair, Corera might have added the vast expansion of CCTV coverage, which helped to identify the GRU officers responsible for this attack.

Anatoly Dobrynin, Soviet Ambassador to the United States, 1962–86

but usually have separate communications and separate budgets, and tend to be generally semi-detached. The legendary Soviet ambassador to the United States, Anatoly Dobrynin, says that the KGB officers rarely made any contribution to discussion at general staff meetings in his embassy;[24] and in London, as was probably the case in some other capitals, the GRU residency was based in a separate building.

As to the typical diplomatic ranks that disguise intelligence officers, it is impossible to pronounce on this with any certainty without knowing who they are, although the pattern favoured by SIS after the Second World War is probably still not unusual. With the bad experience of the PCO disguise in mind (Box 3.1), an influential official report in 1944 on the future organization of SIS advised that it was important to 'ring the changes' among diplomatic titles for its officers.[25] At first, therefore, they were concealed in a variety of relatively minor positions, among them assistant commercial secretary, press attaché, and vice-consul. Outside recruitment to such positions was in any case quite common, so new arrivals without career pedigrees in the diplomatic or consular service were unlikely to arouse much suspicion. It was not long, however, before more senior positions were also used as cover, as claimed by the SIS officer and KGB double agent, Kim Philby. Philby himself had cover as a first secretary at the British embassy in Turkey while head of the SIS station in that country in the late 1940s; the same rank was customarily held by the chief of the important SIS station in the Beirut embassy in the 1950s and 1960s; while at Paris and Washington the chief of station was usually a counsellor. The more junior David Cornwell, better known as the master of the spy novel, John le Carré, had cover as a second secretary in the British embassy in Bonn in the early 1960s and then briefly as a consul in Hamburg. SIS officers appear, however,

---

24 Dobrynin, *In Confidence*, p. 356.
25 Jeffery, *MI6*, p. 603.

only in exceptional circumstances to have been heads of mission (Box 3.4) and only rarely to have led important embassy sections.

> **Box 3.4 British Consulate-General, Hanoi, during the Vietnam War**
> At least two SIS officers were head of mission (Consul-General) at this post during the Vietnam War: Gordon Philo (aka the novelist 'Charles Forsyte') and Daphne Park. This was an exceptional case because it was the hardest of 'hardship posts' and the consul-general was the only consular officer in the mission; fortunately for them, tours only lasted for six months.

A close cousin of the secret service station in the embassies and consular posts of some states is the science and technology section. This is because S&T intelligence – acquiring industrial secrets for commercial gain by more or less innocent methods – has been of huge importance for many decades. Espionage with this end in view is most commonly practised by states such as Russia, China, France and North Korea that have extensive direct or indirect control of key industries. However, Washington also began to give more attention to S&T intelligence in the late 1970s because by then the USA was contributing less than one-third of S&T advances, whereas in the 1950s it had originated three-quarters.[26]

Under the cover of responsibility for publicizing outstanding research and innovation in its own country and promoting international collaboration in research for the common good, the less innocent S&T section cultivates an agent network, often enough relying chiefly on post-doctoral students, academics and company chief executives in its diaspora community, as well as on local scientists and engineers with whom their own researchers have struck up personal relationships. S&T officers might well be intelligence officers, as they certainly were in Soviet missions in the days of the KGB and probably still are in those of its successor, the SVR.[27] China, for long notorious as a leader in S&T intelligence, is believed to have Ministry of State Security officers in its missions devoted to this work; if they are not intelligence officers, it would be surprising if they did not liaise closely with them. The fact that Donald Trump constantly alleges Chinese culpability in this area does not make the allegation groundless. A sizeable consular post adjacent to a concentration of leading universities and research institutes, as in New England in the United States, or high tech industries, as in Silicon Valley (Box 3.3), is very likely to have an S&T section. The French consulates-general in Boston and San Francisco both have such sections.

---

[26] CIA Science and Technology Advisory Panel, 'S&T Intelligence'.
[27] Run by Directorate T of the foreign wing of the KGB, they were called 'Line X officers' and were usually part of the residency.

Modus operandi

Intelligence officers are often required to take an active hand in shaping events. Variously known as covert action, active measures, special operations or political warfare, this covers a spectrum from the modest to the murderous. As a rule, the contribution of those intelligence officers with diplomatic cover tends to be at the modest end, and they serve instead chiefly as agent recruiters and handlers – 'case officers'; where their own 'illegals' are present, they might also be required to give them support. Furthermore, they do not take serious risks to obtain intelligence from protected sources themselves, except when receiving it from their agents, and this is a process in which various devices of 'tradecraft' are designed to minimise the risk of detection; for example, cut-outs and dead drops. Such discretion does not prevent them from actively seeking information from open sources, and to this end – like any genuine diplomat – perhaps travelling widely; in some circumstances and in some degree, this will also provide a check on the veracity of the intelligence supplied by agents.

The most sought-after agents are 'agents in place'; that is, persons occupying positions of trust in sensitive targets who are persuaded to divulge the secrets that come to them in the course of their work. The means of persuasion are well-known: money, the threat to expose embarrassing private behaviour, and the arousing of known or suspected ideological, religious or ethnic sympathies. But 'agents of influence' – who might also pass over secrets without realizing it – are also prized, which is hardly surprising because one strongly suspected of being an example of this species could even become president of the United States (Box 3.5).

Box 3.5 Trump: Russian agent of influence?

Strong circumstantial evidence, which is believed by those in a position to know, such as former CIA Director John Brennan, suggests that, over the 30 years prior to his election as US president in November 2016, Donald Trump was successfully groomed as an agent of influence by the Soviet, thereafter Russian government. It was a classic KGB joint effort of intelligence officers, co-opted oligarchs, and diplomats in the Washington embassy. Trump was an ideal target: he was a prominent New York businessman when Moscow was keen to deepen economic ties with the USA; better still, shortly after his first visit to Moscow, in 1987, he hinted at presidential ambitions and ran advertisements presaging the 'America first' theme of his 2016 election campaign. He was also comfortable with sharp financial and commercial practices; greedy enough to be susceptible to bribery, defenceless against flattery because of his narcissism, and so notorious a womaniser as to make it likely that engineering *kompromat* – at which the KGB were past masters – would be child's play. By 2016, Russian intelligence probably had a strong hold on Donald Trump, not only through his shadowy business dealings with Russian oligarchs but also because of the evidence thought to be in its hands of his sexual adventures during the Miss Universe beauty pageant in Moscow in 2013. Helping him to win the presidential election was the icing on their cake, not least because earlier Russian attempts to influence such elections – to secure the defeat of Richard Nixon in 1968 and in 1983 to prevent Ronald Reagan from enjoying a second term – had failed.

It is unlikely that any major role was played in Trump's cultivation by the secret intelligence *rezidentury* in Russia's consulate-general in New York and embassy in Washington, most if not all of the members of which would have been well-known to the FBI. In the United States itself, the greater part of the fieldwork was evidently done – and done more or less openly – by the oligarchs

---

and the diplomats. It was the new Soviet ambassador to the UN in New York, Yuri Dubinin (shortly afterwards to be ambassador to the USA) who began the operation, in March 1986, assisted by the younger Vitaly Churkin, who later rose to be Russia's UN Permanent Representative from 2006 until 2017. The key role at the end, however, was played by Sergey Kislyak, the extremely able Russian ambassador to the United States, whose father had been a highly regarded major-general in the foreign intelligence wing of the KGB. Sergey had also enjoyed long postings both at the Soviet mission to the UN in New York and at the Washington embassy before becoming ambassador in 2008.

During and immediately after the presidential campaign in 2016, Kislyak courted Trump and members of his team assiduously: for example, at the candidate's foreign policy speech in Washington in April; at the Republican Party convention in Cleveland in July; in Trump Tower during the transition; and in numerous phone calls with Michael Flynn, who was to be Trump's first national security advisor and whose visit to Russia when he was head of the Defense Intelligence Agency the ambassador had arranged. James Clapper, former DNI, told NBC News in May 2017 that 'he oversees a very aggressive intelligence operation.' Kislyak seems to have thought that the project to help elect Trump had been too crudely executed and therefore invited the damaging exposure that followed. But it is probably going too far to say, as Harding does in his book *Collusion*, that it was a 'tactical triumph' but a 'strategic disaster.' After all, it helped to get Trump elected on a foreign policy platform that was pro-Russian; his new administration featured numerous individuals with strong Russian connections of their own; in his first year in office Trump went out of his way to be friendly and accommodating to the Russian leader, Vladimir Putin; he soon got rid of the Director of the FBI, James Comey, who had shown too much resistance to White House pressure to drop its investigation into his doings; and so far, with the assistance of right-wing media outlets and the Republican-controlled Congressional select committees on intelligence, he has managed to prevent Robert Mueller's investigation into the charges of 'Russia collusion' and obstruction of justice reaching his own door. Following the mid-term elections in November 2018, in January 2019 the House Intelligence Committee fell to Democrat control, so the investigation will be getting closer. The world might not have that much longer to wait for Mueller's final report.

Intelligence officers with diplomatic cover in unfriendly states are usually well-known to or strongly suspected by the local security services. This is because embassies tend to be the object of careful surveillance and diplomatic lists sometimes make it relatively easy to form a shrewd idea of the officers' identities. Anatoly Dobrynin added other reasons why, in his embassy in Washington, KGB officers were easily identified by the FBI. Compared to the genuine diplomats, they had more expensive apartments, private cars, and more money for restaurant entertaining. They also spent far more time 'around town' and showed interest in everything, whereas genuine diplomats were known to the State Department 'through routine working contacts on specific problems.'[28]

While identification of intelligence officers cramps their style, this is normally less serious than might at first be thought. For one thing, being case officers rather than field agents, it is unlikely they will be caught doing anything illegal. It is also difficult for a counter-intelligence agency to keep track of them all if it is under-resourced and the number of intelligence officers in an embassy is swollen deliberately, which was a popular tactic of the former KGB. And such 'legals' are usually tolerated on the basis of reciprocity ('we'll permit yours in reasonable numbers on the tacit understanding that

---

28   Dobrynin, *In Confidence*, p. 356.

you'll permit a similar number of ours'). This is why in 1978 the CIA opposed a request that the Justice Department deny entry visas to known Soviet bloc intelligence officers; to do so, it pointed out, would merely result in retaliation in kind, thereby drastically reducing, if not eliminating, its operational capability in those states.[29] The matter is different if legals are indeed detected in criminal activity themselves or are present in thoroughly alarming numbers; but even then, their fate is only to be PNG-d and sent home.

When posted in an embassy to a friendly and particularly an allied country, however, the balance of intelligence officers' work is often quite different. States spy on their friends as well as their enemies, so they might still be engaged in agent recruitment and handling. But it is common practice for them to give more weight to liaison with one or more elements of the local intelligence community; and, to this end, to 'declare' their true role. Cooperation between friendly intelligence agencies in the struggle against common enemies has long been valued; for example, between the Okhrana and the Sûreté against revolutionaries in Paris before 1917. And today examples are plentiful. The most well-known is the Five Eyes' alliance (see Box 4.4).

Intelligence officers with diplomatic cover who are undeclared but strongly suspected are tolerated not only on the basis of specific reciprocity but also on condition that two other unwritten rules of the game are observed. These are that espionage is never admitted, and that its operatives – whether case officers and their agents or covert action personnel – do not act so clumsily as to attract public attention.

The diplomatic price of diplomatic cover

The invention and growth of secret services might have relieved ambassadors of all practical responsibility for running agents themselves, but only at the cost of giving house room to the thinly disguised personnel of these services, sometimes in large numbers. This often causes tension – sometimes acute – between the diplomats and the intelligence officers. Why should this be so? After all, intelligence officers do work regarded as vital to national security and which sometimes invites personal danger despite their diplomatic protection.

Box 3.6 The Raymond Davis affair, Pakistan 2011
On 27 January 2011, Raymond Davis, a private security contractor employed by the CIA with cover as a member of the administrative and technical staff of the US embassy in Islamabad, shot to death on a busy Lahore street two young (armed) Pakistanis shadowing him on motorbikes; a third (wholly innocent) Pakistani was accidentally run down and killed by a CIA vehicle speeding to their colleague's assistance. Davis was arrested by the police, charged with double murder, and imprisoned for almost 10 weeks until Washington – which insisted he had diplomatic immunity – secured his release. Anti-American sentiment, which was already inflamed by drone strikes against Al-Qaeda and

---

[29]   Memorandum for the Record.

Taliban militants near the frontier with Afghanistan, rose further, and US-Pakistan relations, as the US ambassador Cameron Munter said later, went 'straight to hell'. Neither were they rescued from its fires by the CIA-managed mission that killed Osama bin Laden at Abbottabad, not far north of Islamabad, only a few months later. Munter, who had serious misgivings about the drone campaign and was at loggerheads with the CIA station chief, resigned only half way through his posting.

The most common source of the tension between intelligence officers and real diplomats is the duty of the former to take at least some risks with good relations with the host government; this also applies to defence attachés, as noted in the previous chapter. This is a strong temptation for intelligence officers when they populate an embassy in strength, their funds are lavish, their political support powerful, and their communications with home direct; in short, when they are 'cuckoos in the nest'.[30] In such circumstances, heads of mission might find that the chief of station is the real ambassador. It is notorious that KGB residents were often the de facto heads of Soviet embassies but the phenomenon appears also to have been common in those of the United States (especially in developing countries), and no doubt also in those of many other states. Whether chiefs of station rule the embassy kingdom or are only powerful barons within it, the activities they direct often pose a risk to good relations because all states dislike being spied on and object even more strongly to foreign secret services meddling in their internal affairs. Moreover, receiving states usually have diplomatic and domestic law on their side. When, therefore, the association of a diplomatic or consular mission with espionage or covert action is exposed, trouble is bound to ensue. In hostile states, ambassadors will have to face the 'visceral feelings about the enemy within' it has stimulated, possibly expulsions of their staff;[31] and perhaps greater fury when an important ally is the victim and heads of mission have had no warning.[32] The last was no more eloquently demonstrated than by events in Pakistan in the first half of 2011 (Box 3.6) and in Germany in October 2013, when it was revealed by the German press that the Americans had been tapping the mobile phone calls of German chancellor Angela Merkel, almost certainly from a Sigint post in their Berlin embassy. It seems to have been the US diplomats' demand for no more unpleasant surprises that led to the signing of what DCI Admiral Stansfield Turner described only half in jest as the 'treaty of friendship' between the CIA and the State Department in 1977 (Box 3.7).

---

[30] The cuckoo is a brood parasite that lays eggs in the nest of another species; these incubate faster than those of the host bird and produce beefy chicks which frequently kick out the other eggs they find.

[31] Herman, *Intelligence Power in Peace and War*, p. 191. On the diplomatic downside of 'intrusive' intelligence-gathering – including 'close-range technical collection' – see also pp. 371, 372 and 385.

[32] However, in discussing close international cooperation between intelligence services, Herman revealed 'a tacit professional recognition that cooperation is not necessarily a bar to continued targeting of each other's government, defence forces and the like,' *Intelligence Power in Peace and War*, p. 211; see also Pearce, *Spymaster*, pp. 137, 272, for the penchant of SIS officer and later chief, Maurice Oldfield, for spying on Britain's European allies.

> **Box 3.7 The State-CIA 'treaty of friendship', 1977**
> The 'State-CIA treaty' was signed in the spring of 1977 by Secretary of State Cyrus Vance and CIA Director Adm. Stansfield Turner. The CIA refused to direct their station chiefs to divulge the 'operational mechanics or the identity of agents' to ambassadors because this would increase the risk of exposure and – if such a procedure were to be public knowledge – 'be a severe if not fatal blow' to its ability 'to recruit foreign nationals willing to commit treason against their own government.' This is no doubt why, in publicly discussing the treaty on 25 January 1978, Adm. Turner admitted that it required station chiefs to reveal more to ambassadors – 'but not everything', Adm. Turner's Address – Q&A, 5 [www]. See also Saunders to Vance, 9 Feb. 1978 [www]; and Turner to Vance, 23 Feb. 1978 [www]

When intelligence officers with diplomatic cover are expelled, this is usually justified publicly by the accusation of action 'inconsistent with their diplomatic status.' Even the station chief of a friendly state can fall victim to this fate, as in the case of the head of the Mossad station in Israel's embassy in London when it was learned that some of the Mossad officers responsible for assassinating a leading Hamas militant in Dubai in 2010 had travelled on the forged passports of 12 British-Israeli citizens.[33] If breaking the rule of the game against attracting public attention can result in this sort of reaction, so can breaking the rule against cramming too many intelligence officers into an embassy. This is why in 1971 the British government terminated the London posting of 105 Soviet intelligence officers with diplomatic cover.

Expelling intelligence officers usually leads to a 'tit-for-tat' reaction by the second state – expulsion of the identical number of diplomats of the first. Insulation of the dispute in this way minimizes the chances of broader damage to relations but can have serious drawbacks for both embassies. First, via guilt by association, it brings them into bad odour. Second, it is quite possible that country specialists with local language skills who are not intelligence officers will be deliberately swept up in the exchange; for example, in 1971 the Soviet government's retaliatory expulsions from the British embassy in Moscow included the remaining members of the mission's Russian Secretariat.

Even in the absence of expulsions, in-house intelligence officers might cause difficulties for a mission. Unwelcome attention by the security agencies of receiving states, especially when unfriendly, will probably be invited. This might well happen anyway but the presence of the spooks tends to make it more aggressive. Diplomatic premises are bugged, phone calls tapped, staff followed and sometimes physically harassed, and local citizens actively discouraged from having contact with them. Such actions all became routine in states locked directly in the Cold War, and remain a regular feature of some international relationships today. The known or simply suspected presence of intelligence officers can even stimulate or at least provide a ready pretext for popular hostility and mob attacks on embassies. This was the notorious fate of the US embassy in Tehran, which housed a major CIA station, in late 1979.

---

[33]   *Telegraph*, 25 December 2010.

Matters might not be much better in friendly states, particularly if the mission represents a state sensitive to human rights and the local security service has a well-earned reputation for brutality. As well as attracting criticism at home, liaison between the embassy's intelligence officers and such an agency will complicate the embassy's relations with the local authorities since it will be required to draw attention to human rights abuses, and present an obstacle to any attempt to maintain discreet contact with the opposition.

Finally, there is also unlikely to be a relaxed relationship between intelligence officers and genuine diplomats when the former are also required to keep a close eye on the latter for any sign of political unreliability, as is unfortunately the case in some states.[34]

In sum, whether in unfriendly states or friendly ones with different attitudes to human rights, the effect of giving diplomatic cover to intelligence officers is usually to generate some degree of tension between the real and the fake diplomats, and occasionally to impair – and in extreme cases terminate – pursuit of the legitimate functions of the diplomatic or consular mission.

Repaying the diplomats

With all of these risks to hosting intelligence officers in their missions abroad, why do foreign ministries tolerate the practice? Patriotic sensitivity to the needs of a vital service is an important factor and, where this is absent or weak, crude political pressure from a secret service powerful at home will be sufficient. But there is another very important reason: secret services can repay the diplomats for the favours they receive.

First and foremost, intelligence officers can provide 'diplomatic support', sometimes also known as 'policy support'. This means supplying information – including that obtained by decrypts of top secret, intercepted messages – that can furnish valuable tactical assistance in negotiations on any important subject, especially if it reveals the fall-back position of the other side or some point of personal weakness on the part of one or more of its key officials that can be exploited. Herman guesses that in the early 1990s Western intelligence agencies allocated about ten per cent of their resources to 'tactical support to diplomacy'.[35] To mention just two examples, it is therefore credible that the CIA has 'aided and abetted plenty of negotiations' between Israel and the Palestinians, as claimed by George Tenet,[36] and that successful Sigint attacks on the computers and smartphones of delegates attending recent G8 and G20

---

34 Dulles, A. W., to A. V. Watkins [Chairman, Senate Immigration and Naturalization Sub-committee], 9 May 1953, p. 5, point 5 (CREST) [www]
35 Herman, *Intelligence Power in Peace and War*, p. 54.
36 Tenet, *At the Center of the Storm*, p. 55.

summits are said to have provided welcome real-time information to their 'customers'.[37] Most negotiations of great importance by-pass embassies today but even if their diplomatic staff are not direct beneficiaries of diplomatic support, they are well aware of its value and of the contribution that from time to time is made to it by the intelligence officers in their midst.

Closer to the embassies' immediate needs, intelligence officers can also provide them with valuable practical assistance in critical circumstances; for example, by helping with communications and giving warning of attacks, as in the case of the planned Al Qaeda assaults on US embassies in Albania and Uganda in 1998 probably forestalled by the CIA.[38] Generally skilled at operating in the shadows, intelligence officers can also take the strain from the diplomats by serving as paradiplomats in sensitive relationships. (This is the subject of the final chapter.) Last but not least, the 'platform' provided by embassies and consulates for the conduct of operations by intelligence officers, as well as kindred spirits such as drugs and immigration liaison officers, helps greatly to justify their continued existence: no cuckoos, then fewer, smaller, and less well feathered nests. Some secret intelligence agencies even pay rent to their diplomatic landlords; SIS certainly does so.[39]

With incentives on the part of both diplomats and intelligence officers to live in harmony, peaceful coexistence between them has been reinforced in the liberal democracies by the oversight measures introduced in recent years to curb the occasional excesses of the intelligence agencies, as described at the end of the previous chapter. Elsewhere, there is probably still more of a downside to this relationship for the diplomats than for the spooks. In light of the grisly killing of the Saudi journalist, Jamal Khashoggi, in the Saudi consulate-general in Istanbul in early October 2018 by a hit squad in which intelligence officers are reported to have had a hand, this observation is probably well taken by members of the Saudi diplomatic service.

Main references and further reading

Aid, M., 'Eavesdroppers of the Kremlin: KGB Sigint during the Cold War', in Leeuw, Karl de and Jan Bergstra (eds), *The History of Information Security: A comprehensive handbook* (Elsevier: Amsterdam, 2007)

Andrew, C. and O. Gordievsky (eds.), *Instructions from the Centre: Top Secret Files on KGB Foreign Operations, 1975–85* (Hodder and Stoughton: London, 1991)

Andrew, Christopher, and Vasili Mitrokhin (1999), *The Mitrokhin Archive: The KGB in Europe and the West* (Penguin: London and New York, 1999)

Bar-Joseph, Uri, 'A Question of Loyalty: Ashraf Marwan and Israel's intelligence fiasco in the Yom Kippur War', *Intelligence and National Security*, vol. 30 (5), 2015

---

[37]   *Guardian*, 17 June 2013.
[38]   National Commission on Terrorist Attacks, p. 127.
[39]   ISCP, *Annual Report, 2010–2011*, p. 32.

Berridge, G. R., *The Counter-Revolution in Diplomacy and other essays* (Palgrave Macmillan: Basingstoke, 2011), Ch. 5 ('Specific reciprocity and the 105 Soviet spies')

Berridge, G. R., *Embassies in Armed Conflict* (Continuum: New York, 2012), Ch. 1

Borger, J. *et al*, 'US accuses Israel of spying on nuclear talks with Iran', *Guardian*, 24 March, 2015 [www]

Bower, Tom, *The Perfect English Spy: Sir Dick White and the secret war, 1935–90* (Heinemann: London, 1995)

Campbell, Duncan, 'How embassy eavesdropping works' [www]

'Church Committee': *Foreign and Military Intelligence. Book I. Final Report of the Select Committee to Study Governmental Operations with respect to Intelligence Activities. United States Senate* (U.S. Government Printing Office: Washington, 1976). A very important source [www]

Clinton, Hillary Rodham, *What Happened* (Simon & Schuster: London and New York, 2017), pp. 325–75

Comey, James, *A Higher Loyalty: Truth, lies and leadership* (Macmillan: London, 2018), Chs. 11–14

Corera, Gordon, 'The spies of tomorrow will need to love data', *Wired*, May, 2016 [www]

Corera, Gordon, *MI6: Life and Death in the British Secret Service* (Weidenfeld & Nicolson: London, 2012)

Dobrynin, Anatoly, *In Confidence: Moscow's ambassador to America's six Cold War presidents* (Times Books: New York, 1995)

Duncan Campbell.org, 'Embassy Spying' [www]

Greenwald, Di Glenn and Stefania Maurizi, 'Revealed: How the NSA targets Italy', *L'Espresso*, 5 December 2013 [www]

Guardian, 'The NSA Files' [www]

Hannas, W. C., J. Mulvenon and A. B. Puglisi, *Chinese Industrial Espionage: Technology acquisition and military modernization* (Routledge: London, 2013)

Harding, Luke, *Collusion: How Russia helped Trump win the White House* (Guardian Books and Faber & Faber: London, 2017)

Harding, Luke, 'Revealed: The Secret KGB Family Story Of Russia's Ambassador To The US [Kislyak]' *Huffington Post*, 27 November, 2017 [www]

Herman, Michael, *Intelligence Power in Peace and War* (Cambridge University Press and the Royal Institute of International Affairs: Cambridge, 1996), Chs. 1 and 2

Herman, Michael, 'Diplomacy and Intelligence', *Diplomacy & Statecraft*, vol. 9 (2), July 1998

Intelligence and Security Committee of Parliament, *Annual Report 2012–2013*, 10 July 2013, HC 547 [www]

Jeffery, Keith, *MI6: The history of the Secret Intelligence Service, 1909–1949* (Bloomsbury: London, 2010). The official history. Long on detail, so read from the good index

Kralev, N., 'Diplomacy and Intelligence'. A Conversation with John Negroponte – VIDEO, 30 July 2013 [www]

LSE Media Policy Project, 'Online Surveillance'. An excellent portal to online resources [www]

MacAskill, E. *et al*, 'GCHQ taps fibre-optic cables for secret access to world's communications', *Guardian*, 21 June 2013 [www]

Macintyre, Ben, *The Spy and the Traitor: The greatest espionage story of the Cold War* (Viking: New York, 2018). The story of Oleg Gordievsky, the SIS agent in place in the KGB; authoritative and gripping

Mazzetti, Mark, 'How a single spy helped turn Pakistan against the United States', *The New York Times Magazine*, 9 April 2013

National Commission on Terrorist Attacks Upon the United States, *The 9/11 Commission Report: Final Report of the National Commission on Terrorist Attacks Upon the United States* (U.S. Government Printing Office: Washington D.C., 2004) [www] Chs. 3 and 13

NBC News, 'Meet the Press: Full Clapper', 28 May, 2017 [www]

OSO [Office of Special Operations] FROM JULY, 1946 TO DECEMBER 1946, 8 May 1952, CREST [www]

Porch, D., *The French Secret Services: From the Dreyfus Affair to the Gulf War* (Macmillan: London and Basingstoke, 1996)

Sipher, John, 'The Cipher Brief' [www]

Tenet, George, *At the Center of the Storm: My years at the CIA* (HarperCollins: New York, 2007), Ch. 21

4   Spooks as 'Diplomats'

Intelligence officers in the higher ranks of their organizations frequently serve as 'diplomats' in two capacities: first, as special envoys to hostile states; and second, as builders and managers of international secret service alliances, together with less formal and more numerous 'liaison' relationships. As for the first role, why might they be given such tasks when it surely means 'blowing' their cover and when there are usually so many other officials to choose from, among them senior political advisers and even seasoned diplomats themselves? As for the second, at first glance it might be assumed that this role is accepted solely for the obvious advantages it carries for the secret services; so what, if any, are its broader diplomatic benefits, whether intended or unintended?

Intelligence officers as special envoys

Special envoys, otherwise known as the leaders of 'special missions', are sent abroad to conduct diplomacy with a limited purpose for a limited time, and are recognised in diplomatic law. They are a feature of normal diplomatic relationships but are particularly valuable to the diplomacy between states which are so hostile that they do not enjoy permanent missions. In such circumstances, special envoys are the next-best alternative. They also provide great security for the secrecy of a message, which, in the circumstances, might be of considerable sensitivity. And their use to bear a message underlines the importance attached to it, thereby making it more likely that it will receive high-level attention.

When special missions are employed in diplomacy between hostile states, they are often despatched in secret, and almost always when contacts are at an early stage. The first reason for this is the need to minimise the risk of political sabotage. Public knowledge that a special mission to a hostile state is planned, especially if it is a high-level one rumoured to be seeking a *rapprochement*, is likely to spread alarm among factions at home and allied governments abroad whose interests are locked into the *status quo*. Advance warning of what is afoot permits them time to marshal their forces and nip it in the bud. The second reason for secrecy is the need to guard prestige, which is seriously threatened by appearing as a supplicant at the seat of the rival's power, especially if the mission is a failure. These were the main reasons for the intense secrecy cloaking the highly significant first mission to Beijing in July 1971 of US National Security Advisor, Henry Kissinger.

In light of the above, it is hardly surprising that the use of intelligence officers as special envoys has a history as long as that of secret services. The first of their qualifications for the role is that almost all will have had more or less intimate acquaintance with the world of diplomacy by virtue of serving in embassies under diplomatic cover. A few might even have been genuine diplomats earlier in their careers, a case in point being that of Prince Bandar bin Sultan. Bandar served as Saudi ambassador to the United States from 1983 until 2005, then became a much-travelling secretary-general of his country's National Security Council, before finally – from 2012 until 2014 – adding to this the position of head of Saudi intelligence. Another is Moussa Koussa (Box 4.3).

DNI James Clapper briefing President Obama on N. Korea, 23 November 2010

Box 4.1 James Clapper's secret mission to North Korea, November 2014
At the beginning of November 2014, Washington received strong indications that two Americans serving long prison sentences in North Korea would be released. The only conditions were that the United States should send to fetch them a high-level official bearing a personal letter from President Obama, presumably to demonstrate respect for the DPRK's young leader, Kim Jong Un, and help to confirm his authority at home. The Americans quickly chose James Clapper, a former USAF general, career intelligence officer and DNI since 2010. Together with a small team, he flew secretly to Pyongyang on a US military aircraft a few days' later; some members of Congress were briefed in advance and the governments of Japan, South Korea and China were also notified. Although he had gone with no guarantees of success, Clapper swiftly returned with the released prisoners, this time in public. In light of his later public interviews, he was probably chosen for this mission for the following reasons, in roughly descending order of importance: (i) he was certainly, as requested, a high-level official (ii) as America's 'top spy', it was natural that his North Korean counterparts, General Kim

Prince Bandar bin Sultan meeting Russian president, Vladimir Putin, 14 July 2008

Won Hong, minister of state security and General Kim Young Chol, director of the Reconnaissance General Bureau, would wish to be his interlocutors – as proved to be the case – and that as men in the same business they would more readily come to an understanding on the technicalities (iii) since Clapper was neither a diplomat nor a politician, his selection served to underline the Obama administration's keenness to show the North Koreans that he was not being sent to negotiate wider issues (iv) as an intelligence officer he was nevertheless well qualified to watch and listen for pointers on such matters (v) he was further qualified to do this because in the early 1980s he had served as a director of intelligence for U.S. forces in Korea, and followed developments on the peninsula afterwards, and (vi) seeing the North close up had for long been on his 'bucket list'.

The employment of senior intelligence officers as special envoys has two further advantages that are obvious and one that is perhaps less so. First, on secret missions, their experience makes them the best qualified not only to avoid the danger of exposure to the international press but also to cope with the physical risks of what might well be an intimidating environment. It is interesting in this context that at one tense point during James Clapper's secret mission to North Korea (Box 4.1) he was told by his hosts that he had been 'demoted' from his status as President Obama's envoy since he was unable to discuss wider issues and that – 'the people' being in consequence 'agitated' – his security could no longer be guaranteed.[40]

Second, intelligence officers should have a special knowledge of the latest intelligence on their destination, and might well be familiar with the local language.

---

[40]   Gorman and Entous, 'U.S. Spy Chief Gives Inside Look at North Korea Prisoner Deal'.

These were the chief reasons why SIS officers were used in secret contacts with Iraqi officials in the run-up to the war against Saddam Hussein's regime in 2003 (Box 4.2).

Box 4.2 SIS contacts with Iraq in the run-up to the war in 2003
In evidence to the Iraq Inquiry (the official British post-mortem on the 2003 war), SIS contacts with Iraqi officials in the pre-conflict period were confirmed but all details redacted. Nevertheless, Sir Richard Dearlove ('C') made clear that SIS knew much more than the Foreign Office (which had no embassy in Baghdad) both about Weapons of Mass Destruction (WMD) proliferation matters and Iraq in general – and so implicitly explained why SIS was chosen to send the envoy to meet the Iraqis. Gordon Corera, the leading British writer on SIS, says that the envoy in question was the SIS Controller for the Middle East. Because of the government priority attached to knowing whether or not Iraq possessed WMD, a related factor was that Dearlove was in regular contact and got on well with the prime minister, Tony Blair. In the event, the SIS controller was unable to vouch for the credibility of his Iraqi contact's information, although it turned out to be true; namely, that Iraq had no WMD.

Sir Richard Dearlove: head of SIS, 1999–2004

The third and less obvious advantage of choosing intelligence officers for sensitive special missions is that there is always a good chance it will stimulate the appearance of intelligence officers among those they find themselves negotiating with on their arrival. This is probably because of the fit of the proposed agenda with the remit of the local intelligence services and the keenness of the locals to take the measure of their foreign counterparts. The point is, though, that this means that, as well as being on the same professional wavelength as their interlocutors, the visitors will be holding discussions with individuals who are potentially among the most powerful in the country (see section 'Secret intelligence as secret power' in Chapter 2) and thus those with the power to conclude an agreement. These at any rate are among the most important points to emerge from the episodes described in Boxes 4.1 and 4.3, both of which were successful.

Box 4.3 CIA/SIS team negotiates Libya's agreement to abandon WMD, March–December 2003
Assisted by secret intelligence contacts, Colonel Muammar Gaddafi's 'rogue state' of Libya had been inching towards a rapprochement of sorts with the NATO powers since 1999. But in March 2003, when a US-led attack on Iraq was clearly imminent, the pace quickened. Seeming to fear that he might be next, the Libyan leader sent his son, Saif, to London to inform SIS that he wanted to talk about his own WMD. Shortly afterwards, two SIS officers flew to Libya, where they met Gaddafi himself. This was the start of a lengthy negotiation between a joint CIA-SIS team and a Libyan team led by Moussa Koussa, many years earlier head of the notorious People's Bureau in London but then the head of Gaddafi's own 'External Security Organization'. There were several meetings in a European capital, one in Tripoli attended by Gaddafi himself, two visits to weapons sites and a final negotiating session in London on 16 December at the Travellers' Club, a well-known haunt of diplomats and intelligence officers. Encouraged by a phone call from Tony Blair, on 19 December the Libyan leader publicly announced that he was to abandon his programme to develop nuclear weapons. The quid pro quo was that if this were verified, US sanctions on Libya would be lifted. In the event, most US sanctions had been lifted by September 2004.

By way of a footnote to this episode, in October 2008 and January 2009 Moussa Koussa was himself a special envoy to the UK, the upshot of which was the release from a term of life imprisonment in Scotland of Abdelbaset Ali Mohmed al-Megrahi, the Libyan intelligence officer who had been convicted in 2001 for the bombing of Pan Am Flight 103 over Lockerbie in 1988.

Moussa Koussa

Tradecraft and special knowledge of the proposed negotiating partner are qualities that are particularly appropriate where contact needs to be made with hostile non-state groups, the more so if they have been labelled as 'terrorists'. And it is noteworthy that many of the known instances of 'clandestine diplomacy' have taken place with groups of this sort rather than with states. Instances that are now well known include the contacts of the CIA with the PLO, and of SIS with the Provisional IRA in Northern Island, the Taliban in Afghanistan, and the Palestinian organization, Hamas. The New York Convention on Special Missions is silent on contacts with such entities. More importantly, because of state reluctance to confer any respectability – let alone formal recognition – on them, the maximum secrecy that only intelligence officers can provide is the more essential.

The final point to be made on this subject is that there is an excellent chance that – especially if they are senior figures in their services – the identity of intelligence officers sent on special missions will already be known to the other side, so the argument that using them 'blows their cover' falls away. In any case, intelligence officers are sometimes headquarters-based precisely because their cover has been blown already and they are, as a result, no longer of use in the field.

Secret service alliances and liaisons

Fruitful relationships between the secret intelligence services of different states were slow to develop. Today, however, they are not at all unusual. In fact, in 1996, Herman revealed that at that time Britain had 'relationships of some kind with the intelligence and security organizations of some 120 countries.'[41] But the only one that is both well-known and long-lived is the so-called 'Five Eyes' alliance (Box 4.4). In alliances like this, the agencies cooperate chiefly in order to be able to specialise in what they are good at and then share the total intelligence product. Burden sharing with a common goal in view can also extend to covert action, as provided for in the Four Square Agreement of 1954 between SIS and the CIA, in which the former was to have responsibility for anti-Communist operations in Burma, Singapore and Malaya, the latter to take the lead in the Philippines, with operations to be run jointly elsewhere in the Far East.[42]

Secret service alliances such as these tend to be founded on shared political values, common ethnic roots, the same language, and intimate military co-operation. They are further reinforced by a similar professional culture and sense of community; the former includes a belief that the end justifies the means, impatience with politicians, and a specialised technical language; while the latter is built on the challenge of common technical, security, legal and ethical problems. However, even in such close relationships complete trust is rare, partly because of natural inter-service rivalry and partly because of suspicion that the other lot's security is not as good as one's own.

Box 4.4 The Five Eyes' alliance (FVEY)
Originally composed only of the UK and the USA, this developed during the Second World War, was formalised by an international agreement in 1946, and afterwards was joined by Canada (1948), Australia and New Zealand (1956). It is an agreement to cooperate in the gathering of Sigint, with a division of labour and the product shared; today, the alliance appears in practice to embrace cooperation over other types of intelligence as well. It also provides that no member shall collect intelligence on the others, although this has not been taken seriously for many years. A number of 'third parties' were added much later but cooperation with them is more limited. The 'Nine Eyes' arrived with the addition of Denmark, France, the Netherlands and Norway, and the 'Fourteen Eyes' when Germany, Belgium, Italy, Spain and Sweden were allowed to join. However, the core of the relationship probably remains that between the American National Security Agency (NSA) and GCHQ. The Five Eyes' alliance was not formally acknowledged until 2010 and much more about it was revealed in 2013 by the whistle-blower, Edward Snowden, an employee of an NSA private sector contractor, Booz Allen Hamilton. Exchanges of top secret intelligence within this alliance on the Salisbury (UK) nerve agent incident almost certainly contributed to the joint statement by the US, UK, France and Germany in March 2018 that attributed responsibility to Russia. In its Annual Report for 2016–17, the Intelligence and Security Committee of [the UK] Parliament described it as 'the closest international intelligence partnership in the world' (para. 166).

---

[41]   Herman, *Intelligence Power in Peace and War*, p. 208.
[42]   Pearce, *Spymaster*, pp. 148–9; Jones, '"Maximum Disavowable Aid"', p. 1194.

Looser relationships, for which the term 'liaisons' is commonly employed, tend to be just marriages of convenience in the face of common enemies such as Islamic extremism, and might have roots in the intimate links between former dependencies and imperial states. For example, the Crown Prince of Abu Dhabi, Mohammed bin Zayed, is reported to have long had 'strong' ties with SIS, and a former SIS station chief in Abu Dhabi, Will Tricks, has been one of his closest aides since leaving SIS in 2014.[43] Other liaisons rely heavily on good personal relations between the heads (and other senior officers) of the intelligence services concerned, especially when they are powerful figures at home and remain in office for many years, as in the case of B. N. Mullick of India's Intelligence Bureau and R. N. Kao of its Research and Analysis Wing.[44] Maurice Oldfield of SIS was known for a special talent for cultivating friendships with foreign counterparts – as well as with key political figures such as the Shah of Iran and Lee Kuan Yew of Singapore – and had cemented many of them well before he became the service's chief in 1973.

A particularly good example of liaison based on strong personal relations is provided by that between Israeli and French intelligence, the origins of which predated the emergence of the state of Israel in 1948 and endured until the mid-1960s. This had its roots in a common dislike of the British and a shared interest in the Arab world. It almost completely overlapped with the period from 1948 until 1963 in which one man, Isser Harel, was head both of Israel's domestic security and counter-intelligence service, Shin Bet, and (from 1952) the foreign intelligence service, Mossad.

Another instance is the relationship between the Egyptian General Intelligence Directorate and the CIA, which was particularly close during the long period from 1993 until 2011 in which Omar Suleiman – a bitter enemy of the Muslim brotherhood – was director of the *Mukhabarat*.[45] Leaked US State Department cables also revealed that both the Americans and the Israelis, between whom there was also a close intelligence relationship, were keen for Suleiman to succeed Mubarak as president of Egypt.[46] In his memoirs, CIA Director George Tenet repeatedly emphasises how the CIA's 'War on Terror' before as well as after the 9/11 attacks in 2001 was highly dependent on 'scores of other intelligence services' well beyond the members of the Five Eyes' club. Many of these services, which were chiefly in the Islamic world, could infiltrate terrorist sanctuaries to a degree well beyond the capability of his own organization. In return, the

---

[43] *Guardian*, 27 June 2014 and 23 November 2018.
[44] Banerji, 'Access to political leadership key'.
[45] Tenet, *At the Center of the Storm*, pp. 79, 92.
[46] Smallteacher, 'Egypt – U.S. intelligence collaboration with Omar Suleiman "most successful"'.

Omar Suleiman: Director of Egyptian General Intelligence Service, 1993–2011

Americans provided them with technical assistance, 'analytic training', and a great deal of cash.[47]

Even when not resting on high-level professional friendships, secret intelligence relationships will tend to be strengthened by the presence in embassies of 'declared' intelligence officers with the formal responsibility for liaising with the local intelligence community.

What is the diplomatic importance of such close relations?

First, because they are largely out of sight, secret services can continue to collaborate as usual and thereby help to underpin important diplomatic relationships when these are strained by wide differences over one or more high profile issues. This was certainly true of the Five Eyes' intelligence alliance between Britain and the United States at the time of the Anglo-American tensions over the Suez Canal in 1956 and – during the presidency of Donald Trump – the Paris Agreement on climate change, the Iran nuclear deal, tariff policy, and the Middle East.

Second, intelligence officers might also have a soothing effect when a foreign government believes that the diplomats of a sending state have a prejudice against it. Thus the British Foreign Office for long had the reputation of being pro-Arab and it was for this reason that, after the Suez fighting in 1956, preceding which there was secret Anglo-French collusion with Israel to attack Egypt, the new British prime minister, Harold Macmillan, employed SIS to communicate with the Israelis.

Third, close intelligence relationships discourage the targeting of each other's sensitive points, which could otherwise jeopardise friendly diplomatic relations. This is true despite the tacit professional acceptance that this is not completely forbidden.

---

[47]   Tenet, *At the Center of the Storm*, pp. 121, 127, 129, 149–50, 253.

Fourth, a close relationship can be used discreetly to offer or imply a diplomatic quid pro quo in return for intelligence assistance. For example, it seems highly likely that this was anticipated by the Indian government in using one or other of its agencies – probably naval intelligence and the coastguard – to kidnap and return Sheikha Latifa to her father, the prime minister of its close ally, the UEA, in early 2018.[48]

Main references and further reading

Intelligence officers as special envoys

Beaumont, P., 'Profile: Moussa Koussa', *The Guardian*, 31 March, 2011 [www]

Berridge, G. R., *Diplomacy: Theory and Practice*, 5th edn (Palgrave Macmillan: Basingstoke, 2015), Ch.16

Borger, J., 'Two minutes to midnight: did the US miss its chance to stop North Korea's nuclear programme?' *The Guardian*, 30 March, 2018 [www]

Borger, J., 'Mike Pompeo met with Kim Jong-un over Easter, say US officials', *The Guardian*, 18 April, 2018 [www]

'James Clapper on Global Intelligence Challenges', Meeting with Council on Foreign Relations, 2 March, 2015 [www]. Search 'Pyongyang' to get to the point in the transcript where Clapper gives his account of his secret mission to the DPRK

Martinez, Luis, 'How Clapper's Secret Mission to North Korea Came About', ABC News, 9 November, 2014 [www]

Mendick, R, and K. Willsher, 'Terror chief Mousa Kousa helped secure release of Lockerbie bomber', *The Telegraph*, 5 September, 2009 [www]

Mullen, J. and G. Botelho, 'Two Americans freed by North Korea arrive back in U.S., reunited with families', *CNN*, 10 November, 2014 [www]

Scott, L., 'Secret intelligence, covert action, and clandestine diplomacy', *Intelligence and National Security*, vol. 19 (2), 2004

Young, J. W., *Twentieth-Century Diplomacy: A case study of British Practice, 1963–1976* (Cambridge University Press: Cambridge, 2008), Ch. 5

Secret service alliances and liaisons

Aldrich, Richard J., 'International intelligence cooperation in practice', in Born, Hans *et al* (eds.) *International intelligence cooperation and accountability* (Routledge: Oxford and New York) [www]

Appelbaum, J., 'Edward Snowden Interview. The NSA and Its Willing Helpers', *Spiegel Online*, 8 July 2013 [www]

Bower, Tom, *The Perfect English Spy: Sir Dick White and the secret war, 1935–90* (Heinemann: London, 1995). Has a good analytical index, now quite a rarity.

Banerji, Rana, 'South Asian allies essential for Indian intelligence', *Asia Times*, 11 October 2018

Banerji, Rana, 'Access to political leadership key to India's success in intelligence cooperation', *Asia Times*, 12 October 2018

Dearlove, Sir R., Chief of SIS, Evidence of to Iraq Inquiry, 16 June 2010 [www]

Farrell, P., 'History of 5-Eyes – explainer', *The Guardian*, 2 December, 2013 [www]

Herman, Michael, *Intelligence Power in Peace and War* (Cambridge University Press: Cambridge, 1996), Ch. 12

Iraq Inquiry, 2010. Evidence of SIS 1 [www]

---

[48]   *Guardian*, 4 and 6 December 2018. On the close and valuable ties between India and the UAE, see 'India, UAE sign currency swap deal to boost trade ties', *Gulf News*, 4 December 2018.

Joffe, L. 'Isser Harel' (obituary), *The Guardian*, 20 February, 2003 [www]

Norton-Taylor, R., 'Not so secret: deal at the heart of UK-US intelligence', *The Guardian*, 25 June, 2010 [www]

NSA, 'Declassified UKUSA Signals Intelligence Agreement Documents Available at', 24 June, 2010 [www]

Pearce, Martin, *Spymaster: The life of Britain's most decorated Cold War spy and head of MI6, Sir Maurice Oldfield* (Bantam Press: London, 2016)

Tenet, G., *At the Center of the Storm: My years at the CIA* (HarperCollins: New York, 2007)

The Telegraph, 'Isser Heral' (obituary), 19 February, 2003 [www]

Wikipedia, 'Five Eyes'. See especially the section (with associated links) 'Other International Cooperatives' [www]

Wintour, P., 'Expulsions of Russians are pushback against Putin's hybrid warfare', *The Guardian*, 26 March, 2018 [www]

5   Conclusion

By the time that the resident embassy was well established in the sixteenth century, the ambassador was an important figure in the creation and running of secret agent networks, although in some states he played second fiddle to a home-based 'spymaster'. The relationship of the spymaster to his own agents was, however, essentially personal and, partly for this reason, his networks were fragile. Gradually, therefore, ambassadors were given 'secret service' money and largely left to get on with it. Unlike intelligencers, merchants and others, they were uniquely well suited to the task: they had ready access to those with the secrets most worth penetrating; experience of sending information home as quickly and securely as possible; and, under the developing law of nations, growing immunity from prosecution in the event they should be caught receiving stolen secrets or fomenting rebellion. By the nineteenth century, however, ambassadors had begun to cool to espionage and political warfare; not only to direct involvement in it but also to the need for it at all. At this juncture on the threshold of becoming members of a self-confident profession of high social status, with its own code of right conduct, diplomats had come to regard themselves as perfectly capable, via charm and good dinners, of gleaning all of those secrets worth obtaining. In extremis, any grubby business needed could be handled at arms' length by a lower ranking officer or consul.

In the last decades of the nineteenth century, which saw intense great power rivalries, technological developments increased the risk of strategic surprise. The result was that military high commands and foreign ministries (if not so much their diplomatic services) began to think that special efforts should be made to obtain intelligence on potential enemies. This in turn led to the regular appearance in the embassy of the military attaché, shortly followed by the creation of military intelligence services, and then to the emergence of separate civilian foreign intelligence services as well. The distinguishing feature of these new services, which set them apart from the spymaster system of earlier centuries and culminated in the idea of the intelligence community, was their bureaucratization. This facilitated the storage, retrieval, analysis, and distribution through government of the increasing flow of information, and also made it easier to manage agent networks. There is no evidence that these developments were at first greeted with anything but a 'whatever next!' scepticism by the all-seeing diplomats but at the least they promised the opportunity to extend even further their arm's length relationship with the 'dirty' world of secret intelligence. In some states, secret services came to wield great political influence.

The demonstrable limitations of technical means of intelligence-gathering have led to a re-discovery of the value of Humint in recent years and thus arrested what might otherwise have been a slow decline in the numbers of intelligence officers sheltering in diplomatic missions, where they have all of the privileges and immunities of genuine diplomats. The diplomatic price of this is sometimes high: like cuckoos in a nest, intelligence officers sometimes throw their weight around inside the mission and create embarrassing disturbances outside. But they can be a diplomatic asset as well, not least by providing tactical support in important negotiations and a valuable argument for maintaining large embassy networks in order to provide 'platforms' for their work. In some circumstances, high-ranking intelligence officers are also well suited to serve as special envoys, while the alliances and looser liaisons they forge help to underpin important diplomatic relationships when these are seriously strained. In the liberal-democracies, parliamentary oversight of the intelligence community now provides some reassurance to diplomats – along with everyone else – that abuses will not be tolerated.

The relationship between diplomacy and secret service is one of mutual dependence. And, since both are vital to global stability – the one concentrating on the settlement of differences and the other on removing the ignorance that breeds fear and false alarms – it is important that this relationship should be well understood. A serious corollary of this for public policy is that governments should be wary of expelling intelligence officers from embassies in droves simply to make a political gesture or because they are unwilling to spend the money on keeping watch over them. It is important to remember that the intelligence gathered by Sigint posts in Soviet missions in the United States made it more difficult for the ideologically blinkered, desk-bound KGB chiefs in Moscow to sustain their belief that America was gearing up for a nuclear first strike; and that it was embassy-based intelligence officers who enabled KGB defector Oleg Gordievsky to make a major contribution to the avoidance of nuclear war in the early 1980s. He did this by cautioning Western leaders to dampen their anti-Soviet rhetoric by convincing them that it was paranoia that was driving Moscow to the catastrophic conclusion that their country's only chance of survival was to pre-empt imminent NATO aggression with a nuclear first strike of its own.

References

Adams, S.; Bryson, A.; Leimon, M.,'Walsingham, Sir Francis (c.1532–1590)', *ODNB*, 2009

Aid, M., 'Eavesdroppers of the Kremlin: KGB Sigint during the Cold War', in Leeuw, Karl de and Jan Bergstra (eds), *The History of Information Security: A comprehensive handbook* (Elsevier: Amsterdam, 2007)

Allen, E. John B., *Post and Courier Service in the Diplomacy of Early Modern Europe* (Martinus Nijhoff: The Hague, 1972)

Andrew, Christopher, *Secret Service: The making of the British intelligence community* (Heinemann: London, 1985)

Andrew, Christopher, *The Defence of the Realm: The authorized history of MI5* (Allen Lane: London, 2009)

Andrew, Christopher and Oleg Gordievsky (eds.), *Instructions from the Centre: Top secret files on KGB foreign operations, 1975–85* (Hodder and Stoughton: London, 1991); published by Stanford UP in 1993 as *Comrade Kryuchkov's Instructions*

Andrew, Christopher and David Dilks (eds.), *The Missing Dimension: Governments and intelligence communities in the twentieth century* (Macmillan: London, 1984)

Andrew, Christopher and Vasili Mitrokhin, *The Mitrokhin Archive: The KGB in Europe and the West* (Allen Lane Penguin Press: Harmondsworth, 1999)

Barkin, Noah, 'Five Eyes intelligence alliance builds coalition to counter China', *Reuters*, 12 October 2018 [www]

Bemis, Samuel Flagg, 'British secret service and the French-American alliance', *The American Historical Review*, vol. 29 (3), April 1924

Berridge, G. R., 'The ethnic "agent in place": English-speaking civil servants and Nationalist South Africa', *Intelligence and National Security*, vol. 4 (2), April 1989

Berridge, G. R., *Gerald Fitzmaurice (1865–1939): Chief Dragoman of the British Embassy in Turkey* (Martinus Nijhoff: Leiden and Boston, 2007)

Berridge, G. R., 'Fitzmaurice, Gerald Henry (1865–1939)', *ODNB*, 2004

Berridge, G. R. (ed.), *Diplomatic Classics: Selected texts from Commynes to Vattel* (Palgrave Macmillan: Basingstoke, 2004)

Berridge, G. R., *British Diplomacy in Turkey, 1583 to the present: A study in the evolution of the resident embassy* (Martinus Nijhoff: Leiden, 2009)

Berridge, G. R., *The Counter-Revolution in Diplomacy and other essays* (Palgrave Macmillan: Basingstoke, 2011)

Berridge, G. R., *Embassies in Armed Conflict* (Continuum: New York and London, 2012)

Berridge, G. R., *Diplomacy, Satire, and the Victorians: The life and writings of E. C. Grenville-Murray*, 2nd ed, revised (DiploFoundation: Geneva and Malta, 2018) [www]

Berridge, G. R., 'The Trump-Russia dossier cannot be dismissed lightly' (12 January, 2017) [www]

Berridge, G. R., 'Trump and Putin: that 'secret meeting' at the G20 dinner (19 July, 2017) [www]

Born, Hans and Ian Leigh, 'Democratic accountability of intelligence services', *Policy Paper 19* (Geneva Centre for the Democratic Control of Armed Forces, 2007) [www]

Bossy, John, *Giordano Bruno and the Embassy Affair* (Vintage: London, 1991)

Bower, Tom, *The Perfect English Spy: Sir Dick White and the secret war, 1935–90* (Heinemann: London, 1995)

Budiansky, Stephen, *Her Majesty's Spymaster: Elizabeth I, Sir Francis Walsingham, and the birth of modern espionage* (Viking: New York, 2005)

Callières, François de, *The Art of Diplomacy*, ed. H. M. A. Keens-Soper and Karl W. Schweizer (Leicester University Press and Holmes & Meier: New York 1983), Chs. 3 and 8 and App. 1 (Keens-Soper on 'The French Political Academy, 1712: A School for Ambassadors')

Chesterman, S., 'The spy who came in from the Cold War: intelligence and international law', *Michigan Journal of International Law*, 2005–6, vol. 27 [www]

'Church Committee': *Foreign and Military Intelligence. Book I. Final Report of the Select Committee to Study Governmental Operations with respect to Intelligence Activities. United States Senate* (U.S. Government Printing Office: Washington, 1976) [www]

CIA Science and Technology Advisory Panel, 'S&T Intelligence: The Intelligence Community's capability to meet new and evolving needs of national policy-makers', 17 September, 1980 [www]

CIA Scientific and Technical Intelligence Committee, 'The Overt Collection of S&T Intelligence', December 1978 [www]

Clinton, Hillary Rodham, *What Happened* (Simon & Schuster: London, 2018)

Cobban, Alfred, *Ambassadors and Secret Agents: The diplomacy of the First Earl of Malmesbury at The Hague* (Jonathan Cape: London, 1954)

Corera, Gordon, *MI6: Life and Death in the British Secret Service* (Weidenfeld & Nicolson: London, 2012)

Corera, Gordon, 'The spies of tomorrow will need to love data', *Wired*, May 2016 [www]

Croft, Pauline, 'Cecil, Robert, first earl of Salisbury (1563–1612)'. *ODNB*, 2004

DeVine, Michael E. and Heidi M. Peters, 'U.S. Intelligence Community Elements: Establishment provisions', *Congressional Research Service*, 27 June 2018 [www]

Dobrynin, Anatoly, *In Confidence: Moscow's Ambassador to Six Cold War Presidents* (Times Books: New York, 1995)

FAS (n.d.), 'Pakistan Intelligence Agencies' [www]

Fischer, B. B., 'Okhrana: The Paris Operations of the Russian Imperial Police' (CIA History Staff Center for the Study of Intelligence: 1997) [www]

Glassman, Matthew Eric and Sarah J. Eckman, 'House Committee party ratios: 98th–114th Congresses', *Congressional Research Service*, 7 December, 2015 [www]

Glenny, Misha, *McMafia: Seriously organised crime* (Vintage: London, 2008)

Gorman, S. and A. Entous, 'U.S. Spy Chief Gives Inside Look at North Korea Prisoner Deal', *The Wall Street Journal*, 14 November, 2014

Graham, David A. (2018) 'Is Money-Laundering the Real Trump Kompromat?' *The Atlantic*, 19 January, 2018 [www]

Grenville-Murray, E. C. (The Roving Englishman), *Embassies and Foreign Courts: A history of diplomacy* (Routledge: London and New York, 1855)

Grewe, Wilhelm G. H., *The Epochs of International Law.*, trsl. and rev. Michel Byers (de Gruyter: Berlin and New York, 2000)

Hammer, Paul E. J., 'Essex and Europe: Evidence from confidential instructions by the Earl of Essex, 1595–6', *The English Historical Review*. vol. 111 (441), April 1996

Haynes, Alan, *Walsingham: Elizabethan spymaster & statesman* (Sutton: Stroud, Glos., 2004)

Herman, Michael, *Intelligence Power in Peace and War* (Cambridge University Press: Cambridge, 1996)

Herman, Michael, 'Diplomacy and Intelligence', *Diplomacy & Statecraft*, vol. 9 (2), July 1998

Horn, D. B., *The British Diplomatic Service, 1689–1789* (Clarendon Press: Oxford, 1961)

House of Lords, Select Committee on International Relations, 'UK foreign policy in a shifting world order', HL Paper 250, 5 December 2018 [www]

Hughes, Michael, *Diplomacy before the Russian Revolution: Britain, Russia and the Old Diplomacy, 1894–1917* (Macmillan: Basingstoke, 2000)

Hutchinson, Robert, *Elizabeth's Spy Master: Francis Walsingham and the secret war that saved England* (Phoenix: London, 2007)

Intelligence and Security Committee of Parliament, *Annual Report, 2010–2011*, July 2011, Cm 8114 [www]

Intelligence and Security Committee of Parliament, *Annual Report, 2016–17*, December 2017, HC 655 [www]

Iraq Inquiry, 'Private Evidence' [www]

Jeffery, Keith, *MI6: The history of the Secret Intelligence Service, 1909–1949* (Bloomsbury: London, 2010)

Jervis, R., 'Reports, Politics, and Intelligence Failures: The Case of Iraq', *The Journal of Strategic Studies*, vol. 29, February 2006 [www]

Johnson, Charles W. *et al*, *House Practice: A guide to the rules, precedents, and procedures of the House* (U.S. Government Publishing Office: Washington, 2017) [www]

Jones, Matthew, '"Maximum Disavowable Aid": Britain, the United States and the Indonesian Rebellion, 1957–8', *The English Historical Review*, vol. 114 (459), November 1999

Khazan, Olga, 'Gentlemen reading each others' mail: a brief history of diplomatic spying', *The Atlantic*, 17 June 2013 [www]

Kynaston, David, *The Secretary of State* (Terence Dalton: Lavenham, 1978)

Langbart, David A., 'Five months in Petrograd in 1918: Robert W. Imbrie and the US Search for information in Russia', *Studies in Intelligence* (CIA), vol. 52 (1), March 2008, Web Supplement [www]

Lee, Sidney, 'Walsingham, Francis (1530?–1590)', *Dictionary of National Biography*, vol. 59 [www]. Superseded generally by Adams *et al* above but has more on secret intelligence and is an interesting period piece.

Leimon, M. and G. Parker, 'Treason and plot in Elizabethan diplomacy: the "fame of Sir Edward Stafford" reconsidered', *English Historical Review*, vol. 111 (444), November 1996

MacAskill, E. *et al*, 'GCHQ taps fibre-optic cables for secret access to world's communications', *Guardian*, 21 June 2013 [www]

MacCaffrey, Wallace T., 'Cecil, William, first Baron Burghley (1520/21–1598)', *ODNB*, 2004

McDermott, James, 'Stafford, Sir Edward (1552–1605)', *ODNB*, 2012

Macintyre, Ben, *The Spy and the Traitor: The greatest espionage story of the Cold War* (Viking: New York, 2018)

Matthews, Owen and Matthew Cooper, 'Spy or Diplomat? Meet Russian Ambassador Sergey Kislyak, the Most Radioactive Man in Washington', *Newsweek*, 22 June 2017 [www]

Mazzetti, Mark, 'How a single spy helped turn Pakistan against the United States', *The New York Times Magazine*, 9 April 2013 [www]

Memorandum for the Record, Justice Department Appropriations Report Language, 8 August 1978 (CREST) [www]

Middleton, C. R., *The Administration of British Foreign Policy, 1782–1846* (Duke University Press: Durham N.C., 1977)

Millotat, C. O. E., 'Understanding the Prussian-German General Staff system', 20 March 1992, Strategic Studies Institute: U.S. Army War College [www]

National Commission on Terrorist Attacks Upon the United States, *The 9/11 Commission Report: Final Report of the National Commission on Terrorist Attacks Upon the United States* (U.S. Government Printing Office: Washington D.C., 2004) [www]. Chs. 3 and 13.

National Research Council, *Intelligence Analysis for Tomorrow* (National Academic Press: Washington DC, 2011)

Office of the Director of National Intelligence, Intelligence Community Assessment: 'Assessing Russian Activities and Intentions in Recent US Elections', 6 January, 2017 [www]. This is the 'declassified version of a highly classified assessment'.

Pearce, Martin, *Spymaster: The life of Britain's most decorated Cold War spy and head of MI6, Sir Maurice Oldfield* (Bantam Press: London, 2016)

Philby, Kim, *My Silent War* (Panther: St. Albans, Herts, 1969)

Porch, D., *The French Secret Services: From the Dreyfus Affair to the Gulf War* (Macmillan: London and Basingstoke, 1996)

Potter, David (ed), *Foreign Intelligence and Information in Elizabethan England* (Cambridge University Press: Cambridge, 2004)

Radsan, A. John, 'The unresolved equation of espionage and international law', *Michigan Journal of International Law*, vol. 28 (3), 2007

Read, Conyers, 'Walsingham and Burghley in Queen Elizabeth's Privy Council". *The English Historical Review*, vol. 28 (109), January 1913 [www]

Read, Conyers, *Mr Secretary Walsingham and the Policy of Queen Elizabeth* (Clarendon Press: Oxford, 1925)

Richter, L., 'Military and Civil Intelligence Services in Germany from World War I to the end of the Weimar Republic', in H. Bungert, J. G. Heitmann and Michael Wala (eds), *Secret Intelligence in the Twentieth Century* (Cass: London, 2003)

Rohde, David, 'Digitizing the CIA', *Reuters*, 2 November 2016 [www]

Roth, Andrew, 'The man who drives Trump's Russia connection', *Washington Post*, 22 July, 2017 [www]

Rule, John C., 'Review of *Espions et Ambassadeurs au Temps de Louis XIV* by Lucien Bély', *The International History Review*, vol. 14 (4), November 1992

Satow, Rt. Hon. Sir Ernest, *A Guide to Diplomatic Practice*, 2nd. rev. ed., vol. 1 (Longmans, Green: London, 1922)

Seligman, Matthew S., *Spies in Uniform: British military and naval intelligence on the eve of the First World War* (Oxford: Oxford University Press, 2006)

Senate Judiciary Committee, Interview of: Glenn Simpson, 22 August, 2017 [www]

Smallteacher, R., 'Egypt-U.S. intelligence collaboration with Omar Suleiman "most successful"', *Wikileaks*, 1 February, 2011 [www]

Smith, David and Spencer Ackerman, 'Who is Sergey Kislyak, the Russian ambassador rattling Trump's presidency?', *Guardian,* 3 March, 2017 [www]

Spiegel Staff, 'Embassy Espionage: The NSA's Secret Spy Hub in Berlin', *Spiegel Online International*, 27 October, 2013 [www]

Steele Dossier [www]. For original posting in Buzzfeed [www]

Steele, J., 'Vitaly Churkin obituary', *Guardian*, 21 February, 2017 [www]

Stockwell, John, *In Search of Enemies: A CIA story* (Futura: London, 1979)

Stone, Lawrence, *An Elizabethan: Sir Horatio Palavicino* (Clarendon Press: Oxford, 1956)

Swaine, Jon and Shaun Walker, 'Trump in Moscow: what happened at Miss Universe in 2013', *Guardian*, 18 September, 2017 [www]

Szechi, Daniel (ed), *The Dangerous Trade: Spies, spymasters and the making of Europe* (Dundee University Press: Dundee, 2010)

Taylor, P., 'Iraq war: the greatest intelligence failure in living memory', 18 March, 2013, *Telegraph* [www]

Tenet, G., *At the Center of the Storm: My years at the CIA* (HarperCollins: New York, 2007)

U.S. House of Representatives, Permanent Select Committee on Intelligence, *Interview of: Glenn Simpson*, 14 November, 2017 [www]

'VCDR', United Nations, *Treaty Series*, vol. 500 [www]

Wicquefort, Abraham de, *The Embassador and His Functions*, trsl. Mr Digby (London, 1716)

Wikipedia, 'Agent of Influence' [www]

Wikipedia (n.d.) 'Francis Walsingham'. This carefully written, authoritative and up-to-date piece is available online

Wilson, Derek, *Sir Francis Walsingham: A courtier in an age of terror* (Carroll & Graf: New York, 2007)

www.ingramcontent.com/pod-product-compliance
Lightning Source LLC
Chambersburg PA
CBHW041540120626
46551CB00019B/2784